Look What Some People Are Saying...

"All parents want to give their kids the best. *The Gift of Enough* challenges parents to rethink their understanding of BEST and to embrace the concept of giving their kids "enough". Parents will be encouraged and equipped on this road to contentment and gratitude."

–Jim Bob and Michelle Duggar, Parents of 19 Kids

"With warmth, wit, and wisdom from her own experiences, Marianne Miller gifts us with an outstanding book every parent must read to make life more fulfilling and meaningful for kids in our materialistic culture."

–Gloria DeGaetano, Author of *Parenting Well in A Media Age*

"Remember *What to Expect When You're Expecting?* Every mom on the planet read that book to prepare for pregnancy and childbirth. Now Marianne Miller has written a parenting book to help parents teach proper attitudes about money and possessions. In a culture of excess, she speaks truth and reason and balances it with everyday stories and practical help. I wish I'd had this wonderful reference when my children were young, but you can bet I'll get it for them to use when they raise my grandchildren!"

–Leslie Wilson, Speaker, Author, Editor

"Packed with wisdom and practical ideas, *The Gift of Enough* equips and empowers parents to raise children who appreciate all they have without relentlessly pursuing more."

–Jill Savage, Founder and CEO of *Hearts at Home*

"Now, before it's too late, give the gift of "enough" to your kids. Readers of *The Gift of Enough* can do more than climb out of debt themselves—they can raise a generation of kids who never get into debt in the first place! Marianne Miller offers solid ideas for teaching kids to walk away from excess and save for what they truly want. This book will empower parents, who in turn can empower their kids to look around and see they have enough, more than enough."

–Ann Kroeker, Author of *Not So Fast*

"Would you like your children to experience peace? To be content? Then you must read *The Gift of Enough*. Marianne's analysis of the culture and how it influences children's opinions of what is enough is compelling. Her insights are extremely timely and urgently needed because of our culture of entitlement. Your children can become more grateful and joyful than they are now and content when they're adults. What a gift you'll give them! Her examples are purposeful, helpful, and engaging. Her writing is crisp and full of humor. I'll be recommending this book to many!"

–Kathy Koch, Ph.D.,
President of Celebrate Kids, Inc., and Author of *Screens and Teens: Connecting with Our Kids in a Wireless World*

"Of the hundreds of clients we serve across the country, Marianne is the one to whom we turn when families need help with kids and money...in a word, it's her 'superpower'."

-Craig Westrick and Layne Hoekema,
Sr. Financial Advisors, Ronald Blue & Co.

"You'll laugh out loud as you learn from Marianne's real-life stories and honest advice. Marianne's combination of honest storytelling and practical wisdom offers parents simple, effective ideas they can begin using today."

–Anita Lustrea, Executive Producer
and Host of Moody Radio's Midday Connection.

The Gift of Enough

Raising Grateful Kids
in a Culture of Excess

ECC 5:10 Marianne Miller

MARIANNE MILLER

WESTBOW PRESS
PRESS
A DIVISION OF THOMAS NELSON
& ZONDERVAN

WestBow Press books may be ordered through booksellers or by contacting:

WestBow Press
A Division of Thomas Nelson & Zondervan
1663 Liberty Drive
Bloomington, IN 47403
www.westbowpress.com
1 (866) 928-1240

ISBN: 978-1-4908-6467-9 (sc)
ISBN: 978-1-4908-6468-6 (e)

Library of Congress Control Number: 2014922983

Printed in the United States of America.

WestBow Press rev. date: 2/16/2015

To Andy—for freeing this book from the recesses of
my mind and supporting me on this journey.

To Michael, Bryan, Christopher, and Matthew—for sharing ice
cream cones, splitting Happy Meals, skipping the carnival rides,
ordering water at restaurants, and never holding it against me!

Contents

Introduction

I grew up in a frugal family. As a young girl I simply viewed my parents as prudent, but as I reached an age of greater social awareness I came to understand that others considered us cheap. I began to notice chuckles and elbow nudges, visitors signaling they couldn't wait to talk about us on the drive home.

I imagined their comments, "Can you believe how cold it was in that house? You could hang meat in there."

"I know, and did you see the armrest of that junky chair fall to the floor when I put my weight on it?"

By the time I entered high school, my dad had risen to senior vice president of the company where he worked his entire career. Multiple promotions over the years resulted in several moves, and we finally settled in one of the wealthiest cities on the East Coast. Nevertheless, Dad continued to push-mow our lawn, even though landscaping companies meticulously maintained every surrounding yard. We grilled hamburgers more than steaks and never imagined we could leave a room without turning off the lights. Naturally, our family's frugality extended to our modes of transportation. While some of my classmates drove the brand new cars they got for their sweet-sixteen birthdays, my brother and I shared a rusted, pink Chevy Nova—the passenger door secured with a rope.

Not until I became an adult did I fully appreciate the gift my dad had given each of his five children: He helped us understand the concept of Enough. He guided us to become secure in who we were as individuals and debunked the myth that success in life depends upon the opinions of others. He showed us that going to the park together nearly every Sunday far outweighed any material thing he could give us, that spending time together as a family would mean more and last longer than clothes or cars or fancy meals. As I look back nearly five decades removed from the foundation Dad laid, I realize that the gift of Enough empowered me to enjoy life with an unsurpassed freedom. The sweet joy of contentment transcends the lies culture whispers regarding possessions. Passing the baton of this simple principle to future generations ranks among the greatest gifts I can give to my kids.

My story is unique to me; not everyone grew up as I did. But every individual falls along a spectrum of thriftiness to indulgence. So whether your parents practiced frugality like mine or were more extravagant, each of us has foundational beliefs about money and possessions, shaped by our family of origin and by our culture. Some of us grew up with parents who never spoke about money, while others have a history of hearing Mom and Dad fight about spending. Understanding our financial history helps us solidify who we are today and what we want to teach our children.

Regardless of how you were raised, and regardless of mistakes you've made in the past, we can all start fresh with our children and free multiple generations from the stress that accompanies chasing what culture says we should pursue. Give yourself freedom to leave past mistakes or ideologies behind and focus instead on the things you can do today.

As my husband, Andy, and I considered what we wanted for our four boys when they ventured out into the world, we looked to our many years of experience as financial counselors with Crown Financial Ministries to guide our thinking. Crown is an international organization founded by Larry Burkett to share biblical principles about money through small groups, seminars, and coaching. We have counseled hundreds of families over the past decade, and in our work we have observed quite a few similarities in the families who have found themselves in the deepest trouble.

When we began serving with Crown, we assumed we would be counseling impoverished families. What we discovered was that the majority of those who sought assistance were families with significant incomes. Why, we wondered, were these high-income earners in trouble? I examine the answer in Chapter 2.

My heart for writing this book comes as the direct result of working with families who have allowed us to accompany them on their journey. My heart breaks when I see couples juggling debt, working extra hours and extra jobs, and trying desperately to manage the stress, but I have also seen outstanding victories when couples are willing to do the hard work to break old habits. My heart also aches for the families who may not be in any financial trouble at all, yet they struggle to understand why their kids aren't grateful, even though they have so much.

We have learned that if families can establish their definition of Enough and work as a team to embrace contentment, they are rewarded with both freedom and peace. And we can certainly pass along that message to our children, so that they, too, can become grateful for all they have received.

CHAPTER 1

UNSOLICITED ADVICE FROM A STRANGER

I'd been warned. Over the years Andy, my husband of 26 years, has had to frequently remind me that strangers are not always receptive to my random conversations. He has said that people in check-out lines or toy aisles or those attending sporting events didn't go there looking to make a new friend or gain some new insight, so I should just stay silent. Sure, that makes sense.

But what if they *need* encouragement and insight? What if a few words might cause them to see their child or their situation in a new way? When a young mom has that embarrassed, frustrated look on her face as she wrestles a thrashing toddler off the floor and into the shopping cart, I think she *wants* to hear, "He's two. This is his job right now to figure out that things don't always go his way. Your behavior is appropriate, and his will be, too—just not today."

I think I talk to strangers so easily about their kids because, a long time ago, someone helped me in a moment of emotional frailty. Mere weeks post-partum with my firstborn, I boldly ventured to Wal-Mart to get a few essentials. I remember thinking, "Look at me, World—I just gave birth to a brand new human being, and now I have left the security of my home with this tiny bundle to accomplish some brave tasks and—" Just then the front wheel of

1

my shopping cart locked up. No matter how much I pushed, lifted, and maneuvered it still wouldn't go. No problem, I decided to just lift my precious, sleeping baby out of the malfunctioning cart and find one that worked.

But the infant seat, which fit onto the cart so easily, would not release. I pushed and prodded and pulled harder, but it remained attached to the broken cart. All the shaking woke baby Michael, who naturally began screaming the scream that causes people to turn their heads and wonder, "Why is that baby crying? Who would take a baby so young out to Wal-Mart? What kind of mother can't quiet her own child?"

Thoughts like these increased my panic. Just as I fantasized about lifting the entire cart into the back of my van to escape the nightmare, an older woman approached. She was too old to know the mechanics of the new-fangled infant seat, but she was wise and bold enough to talk with me: "Babies cry." Two words, a nod, and a kind smile. What truth! I wanted to hug her right there in the produce section. Babies do cry. I am a good mom. Babies can leave the house and live. The two of us managed to pry the infant seat out of the cart, and I continued shopping with a renewed sense of confidence and the beginning of a passion for helping young moms.

It has been eighteen years since that interaction in Wal-Mart, yet I have never forgotten how much my attitude changed in that moment through the simple words of a stranger. No longer was I a bad mom; I was simply the loving mom of a baby who cried. Babies cry. Within six years after that shopping horror, I had given birth to four boys—who all cried. But I was emotionally ready for them.

So yes, I'm that stranger who might nod in empathy and offer a word or two, despite my husband's cautions. I always hope people don't feel judged. But we live in a culture that seems to just be waiting to feel judged by others. I think this has become worse with the increase of reality television shows. Just think, for entertainment we sit back on our couches and watch someone else's "real" life.

We eat our popcorn and wonder, "Do people really live like this? I wouldn't do that. That's weird."

So when our own child starts acting up in public, we feel the stares and we assume judgment by strangers—perhaps even where there is none. Or maybe there really is judgment in the stares, but that shouldn't matter. My child throwing a fit does not make me a bad mom; it simply makes him a child who has much to learn. When we feel judged, we can mistakenly parent to simply stop the attention-getting behavior of our child, thereby stopping the judgment. Give the child what he's crying for so at least I won't be stared at. Wow, that's a lot of power for a three-year-old to wield! A parent who caters to a crying child has now delayed teaching for another day. And on that future day, the lesson will be slightly more difficult to teach than it would have been the day before.

Just prior to beginning this book, I witnessed such a scene. A young mom shopped at Target with a sleeping baby in the infant seat, a toddler in the shopping cart itself, and a child about four, who grabbed random toys down the aisle. "Can I get this? How 'bout this? You promised last time . . . " Certainly outnumbered, her words carried no clout, especially when the toddler in the cart chimed in with her inharmonious whine for a new doll. I casually paused to provide reinforcements if necessary. The mom whispered through clenched teeth, "We bought something last week, so not this week. Stop whining." The older child ramped up his demands with an unholy shout, "But I waaaaant thisssss!" combined with a half-hearted kick to his mom's shoe.

I sensed the mother wavering. I heard my husband's warnings rolling around in my head. Regardless, I opened my mouth: "Stay strong! He looks like a boy who has enough toys already." Rather than feeling judged, this mom welcomed the support. She stood a little taller and spoke with more conviction, "You heard me. Put it back. We're leaving." Rather than leaving, however, she and I commiserated about "kids these days" and the amount of stuff they all have. I talked with her about my many experiences counseling families in financial trouble and about my own struggles with teaching my four boys not to chase "stuff" and to be content and grateful for everything they have. We talked about delayed gratification, allowances, keeping junk out, and the importance of family bonding. She genuinely appreciated the new insights. Just before we parted she said, "Maybe you should just write a book."

I had never really thought about writing a book before that day, but it made sense. While books about teaching kids to be financially wise are plentiful, I have not found one yet that speaks parent to parent about the struggles of doing so in a culture that's fighting against us. We want kids to be responsible with money, yet if we don't prepare them specifically for life in our materialistic culture, we set them up for financial struggles and a life marred with discontentment.

> *We want kids to be responsible with money, yet if we don't prepare them specifically for life in our materialistic culture, we set them up for financial struggles and a life marred with discontentment.*

This book is not about saying, "Thank you" and writing thank you notes. While that's a start, kids can do these pleasantries and still not experience true gratefulness or contentment. For over a decade, my husband and I have very purposefully focused on raising our four sons to be grateful and content with what they have. At times, it's been challenging to swim against the tide of materialism. But swim we have. And we've not been alone. Our kids were actually not the only kids in their middle school to have no cell phone or social media or other random cool stuff. Other families also opted out. What we found interesting, though, was that our kids rarely even asked for these things. Weird? Unbelievable? Not really, when you consider that we've had the benefit of a behind-the-scenes look into the financial lives of hundreds of high-income families who all experienced incredible strain financially. As it turns out, money and material possessions actually don't ensure a happy life. We knew it and our kids knew it.

As you peruse the pages of this book, remember I'm merely offering a collection of insights, real-life stories, a few studies, and some practical ideas. Take what sounds good to you. Leave what seems too extreme. But be encouraged that you are not alone. Be convicted to make changes that could make your life less stressful and your kids more grateful. I hope you never feel judged. Sure, a child can have a cell phone in middle school and still be grateful. Your Christmas tree can be surrounded by a mountain of gifts, which can all be received and cherished with gratitude. But if your kids don't seem grateful or content, they may have to wait until their attitudes change to receive these gifts.

Before you talk to your kids about excessive toys and trinkets, or about contentment and happiness, or about chasing the latest and greatest, it helps to understand how "The Joneses" really live.

CHAPTER 2

THE JONESES ARE BROKE

"My wife wanted us to call you about our finances. We're actually in pretty good shape, but I wouldn't mind getting a little advice from you on retirement." This opening statement introduced us to one of the first couples we counseled, who I'll call the Joneses. Crown Financial Ministries referred them to us shortly after Andy and I became certified financial counselors.

Mr. Jones, who had an Ivy League MBA, earned six-figures as the CEO of an international corporation. As we gathered data in our initial meeting, we realized that an income many would consider abundant was not enough to support his family. He owed nearly a year's salary in school debt. He had maxed out a variety of credit cards, and he was frantically trying to roll his first and second mortgage together to reduce his monthly payments.

Mr. Jones consistently charged new credit cards to make the minimum payments on the cards he had already maxed out. In our fourth week of counseling, he shared that they had hit a stumbling block with the credit card shuffling. My husband inquired whether the couple had any further outstanding debts that weren't on the summary sheet he had prepared.

"Well, there's one more small loan," he said. As we questioned him about the balance, interest rate, and duration, he shared that his American Express Gold card required payment in full each month. In order to retire the balance, he had borrowed "just a couple hundred or so" from the cash his daughter had accumulated from four years of babysitting. "I'm paying her a fair rate of interest, so it's a win-win for everyone," he said. We saw his wife's jaw drop and realized she had no idea their predicament was so dire.

My husband and I met with the Joneses every few weeks for several months. Unfortunately, we made little progress. We found it challenging to make headway with them because despite being in a financial mess, they constantly pursued the next purchase. Mr. Jones didn't feel that he had enough because he did not understand the concept of Enough.

Over the last decade, we have counseled hundreds of families like the Joneses—all earning high incomes, all living beyond their means. From the outside, everything looked perfect. But their neighbors never saw what we saw—stress, anxiety, fear. Nice cars and nice homes fooled them. Being fooled means they, too, may have been tempted to step outside the safety of their incomes and live off credit—money that was not really theirs to spend.

When Upton Sinclair wrote *The Jungle* in 1906, exposing the unsanitary conditions inside Chicago's meat packing industry, it changed the way people felt about the meat they ate. After people read, "This is no fairy story and no joke; the meat will be shoveled into carts and the man who did the shoveling will not trouble to lift out a rat even when he saw one," [1] it was probably more challenging for them to enjoy that once-tasty hamburger.

Likewise, having seen the stressful reality behind these families' beautiful façades, I feel compelled to expose the lie that promises us that chasing these things is a worthy pursuit that will bring joy. By working with and studying these families who were in deep trouble, we noticed they possessed many predictable similarities. These traits include: having a false sense of security, pursuing the next thing, living without a plan, and lacking a healthy fear of debt.

A False Sense of Security

Mr. Jones, with his MBA and high salary, wasn't the only person we counseled who failed to recognize that a financial problem existed. His wife knew, but he didn't. Why? In so many of the families we worked with, one or both of the spouses had no idea their situation was dire. Often couples would make the appointment with hope that we would use our magical powers to help them find money to pay their bills. They wanted help with the symptoms (significant debt load and stress) of their problem (overspending) without having any idea that a real problem existed. This fruitless exercise would be like going to the doctor to get strong medicine to stop headaches caused by a brain tumor.

Perhaps because these individuals surrounded themselves with new cars, nice homes, and extensive wardrobes, they didn't recognize that a problem even existed. "How could anything really be wrong if I pull into this neighborhood every night driving this car?" they wondered. When they felt stressed, they frequently bought something new as a way of self-soothing. "See, it's not so bad. I can afford this new watch." But they couldn't afford it. The reality of their situation was that they were teetering on the edge of a cliff, rocks crumbling beneath their feet, and yet they believed they were "on top of the world."

Even those families who didn't make six figure incomes could fool themselves into believing they didn't have a real problem. Mere access to credit either from credit cards or second mortgages can mask the truth that they are living beyond their household income. I remember one mom of four who commented after taking a serious look at her family's fixed expenses, "I didn't realize that I really couldn't afford to be going to Starbucks once a week or buying $20 shampoo and conditioner. I didn't even think about whether we had the money for it or not. I just assumed we did."

I am probably not the only one who has personally torn up nearly a million dollars in offers over the past decade—offers from banks hoping to extend cash for anything we might need. Such offers of help sound so friendly. They never mention the fact that we must pay the banks back considerably more than they loaned us, but that's just a technicality. Prior to the recession of 2008, radio ads from banks would frequently entice people to dream: "What would you do with $25,000? Remodel your kitchen? Take that dream vacation you always wanted?" The ads implied that the equity in your home was just being wasted. Why not use this equity to make yourself happy?

One mortgage broker explained that he had quite a few clients who would use their house as a piggy bank, getting money out every time it appraised higher. It became so easy for families across America to get caught up in the nation's prosperity and forget that living beyond their means was dangerous. After the start of the recession, banks began to realize that giving people money wasn't always the best idea for them or their customers.

Pursuing the Next Thing

The title of this book refers to the gift we give our children when they understand how much is enough. The Bible is definitive: "Whoever loves money never has enough; whoever loves wealth is never satisfied with their income. This too is meaningless" (Ecc. 5:10 New International Version). [2] The couples who outspent their high incomes did not understand the concept of Enough. They wanted

> *Whoever loves money never has enough.*

more—a more expensive house, fancier vacations, more jewelry, more shoes, more fashion, more technology, and more entertainment.

Yet many families who earn more simply spend more. Despite annual salary increases, a PNC branch banker commented, "Most people keep their debt ratio about the same. As their salaries increase, they simply increase the loans on cars and houses, never paying anything off."

By always seeking more, families like the Joneses don't recognize the abundance they have been given. When people are asked, "How much money do you need so that you will have enough?" they respond consistently that they need about 10% more than they currently earn. This amount holds true no matter how much they made initially. It seems ingrained in our human nature to want more than we already have.

We want more, so we obtain more, but do we enjoy more? I love Fourth of July celebrations. I love the tradition of picnics at the park followed by fireworks at dusk. But what if our town put on a fireworks show every Saturday night? What if they had fireworks every day? At some point the excitement of the fireworks would diminish. The experience would no longer be special; it would simply be a routine part of our day. Imagine if the stars in the sky only appeared one night a year, what a glorious event that would be! Yet, if I'm honest, I rarely ever look up even on the starriest of nights.

We become conditioned by what we see around us. After only a short time, the formerly exciting and new things become ordinary and old things. We dream about and shop for and drive that new luxury car, but after awhile it has a sticky steering wheel and muddy floor mats just like the old car. Not understanding Enough kept the Joneses seeking more and feeling less satisfied and more stressed. Not appreciating what they already had left them feeling empty.

In a study conducted by *The New York Times* and Harvard student Jordi Quoidbach, chocolate lovers ate a piece of chocolate and then promised to abstain for the rest of the week. Another group pledged to eat as much chocolate as they comfortably could and were even given a mammoth two-pound bag of chocolate to help them. When they returned the next week for another chocolate tasting, the people who ate as much as they wanted enjoyed the new chocolate much less than they had the week before.

Those who had given up chocolate in between were the only ones who enjoyed it as much the second week as the first. Temporarily giving up chocolate, even when they had the cash to buy all they wanted, renewed their enjoyment of this special treat.[3] **If we want our kids to enjoy life more, then we may actually need to give them less.**

The Apostle Paul writes in Philippians 4:12 "I know what it is to be in need, and I know what it is to have plenty. I have learned the secret of being content in any and every situation, whether well fed or hungry, whether living in plenty or in want." It didn't matter if Paul was well fed and experiencing a time of plenty. He still had to learn to be content. He admits that his human nature was to be discontent.

Clearance racks and steep discounts also woo people to continue to purchase the next thing. How many times have you heard someone say, "I had a 50% off coupon, so I had to use it." I know I've said it. But isn't 100% off even better? Certainly using coupons for things you *need* to buy is a great idea, but more often they provide just enough temptation for people to rationalize a purchase by citing the amount they are "saving" rather than considering the amount they are spending. Coupons, sales, and clearance racks certainly aid in our pursuit of the next thing to buy.

No Spending Plan

Living paycheck to paycheck is the norm for close to 76% of Americans. Fixed expenses and daily living absorb most of the money from each paycheck. Online lender CashNetUSA said 22% of the 1,000 people it recently surveyed had less than $100 in savings to cover an emergency, while 46% had less than $800.[4] After paying debts and taking care of housing, car and child care-related expenses, the respondents said there just wasn't enough money left over for saving more.

But when paychecks total thousands of dollars every few weeks, shouldn't that be enough? It's not. A branch manager in one affluent community remarked, "I watch the accounts in here rise every Friday, and then, within two weeks, most are down to almost nothing. We get some pretty significant deposits in this bank, but they are still gone by the end of the month." How easy it can be to fall into this cycle!

Most families live this way because they have no active budget. They may record what they spent each month, but they do not actively assign their dollars a specific place to go. They don't plan for the car to need repairs or the water heater to stop working. Diligently recording where the money goes is nothing but a passive activity. A "recorder" spends money without forethought, only afterthought. Understanding the difference between *recording* where the money went and *planning* where the money is to go is critical for families. One is reactive, while the other is empowering.

Families who don't actively budget also have no specific plan for saving money to pay for braces, college, or retirement. Instead of making decisions now for later, they assume they will figure it out when the time comes. At the orthodontist's office, I once saw a woman who carried a $2,000 purse yet complained about how long it would take to pay off the braces. Perhaps the purse was a fake, and maybe her diamond earrings were fake, too, but if they were real, not buying them would have paid for the braces and perhaps eased some stress. One pharmacist we counseled had to add extra shifts for two years in order to pay off his daughter's braces.

Unfortunately, not planning is the most common cause for the accumulation of credit card debts. These debts usually don't result from a year-long job layoff, but instead they steadily grow over time as the family consistently spends more than they make and uses credit cards to make up the difference. Once they fail to pay off the balances each month, fees and interest begin to accumulate on top of the initial debt. Sometimes if the family makes only minimum payments each month, the debt might never be paid off because only the interest is paid rather than any of the principle.

No Healthy Fear of Debt

Our culture so readily accepts mortgages, car loans, student loans, and credit card debt that it's easy to forget that debt equals bondage. However, the Bible's wisdom is quite clear: "The borrower is slave to the lender" (Proverbs 22:7). The people my husband and I met with who were in debt lived in bondage. Sadly, many didn't realize it because they had found security in surrounding themselves with their stuff. They carried large debts, but thought they could "afford" the payments—at least until an emergency occurred. Or a job loss. Or a medical crisis. Usually, it wasn't until the money ran out or one spouse wanted to leave their job that they realized they were indeed trapped—and had limited options.

By avoiding debt, people can increase their options and freedom in life. I remember the first time I realized that some people didn't have car loans. As a naïve 25-year-old, I assumed that everyone my age had one until my friend Anne told me she was saving up money to pay cash for her next car. I didn't even know you *could* pay cash. I pictured her carrying her pile of $100 bills into the car dealership and plopping the money down on the counter.

Once Andy and I began to consider the possibility of paying off our cars, we focused our budget in that area and paid off both cars in three years. Once we owned the vehicles free and clear, we put the same amount of money into an account to pay cash for the next car. Living without car payments felt so good that we focused our resources on the mortgage and, after twelve years, paid it off as well. Granted, this was only possible because it was a modestly-priced home when we bought it. Many in the financial world think it's foolish to pay off a mortgage for a number of valid reasons. But the freedom and relief we have experienced living without a mortgage is worth the supposed stigma of being foolish.

The reality, however, for most of the people we counseled was that they bought a new car—one the car salesman promised them they could afford. Then, they drove it until they grew tired of it or saw a new one they liked better. Since they hadn't yet paid off their loan, the friendly car salesman helped them roll it into another loan for the new car. The cycle continued with the loan never being paid off.

We recently got a call from our car dealership informing us that someone had come into the dealership and wanted to buy our used car. The salesperson informed us that we could get a new car for the same payments we were currently paying. When we told the caller we didn't have a loan with them, they said there had been a mistake and there really was no buyer for us. Tricky, wasn't it—offering up the temptation of a brand-new car and implying that it would be the same price as the used car? But this kind of practice happens all the time.

Lessons for Our Children

By looking more closely beneath the surface of our culture and considering these common traits, we can raise our children to confidently navigate their financial futures with contentment and peace. When Andy and I started counseling people about their finances, we were raising four young boys ages one to six years old. It didn't take long before we looked at each other and asked, "What can we do right now to train these boys so they will not end up living in the stress-filled situations that so many families find themselves in?" After hours of discussing what we had witnessed first-hand in counseling and what we already saw in the "I-want-that" world of little kids, we decided to make some changes.

First, we admitted that no amount of money the boys would ever earn would be enough for them, if they didn't understand how much was enough. Often parents push for good grades to secure a good college to secure a good job to secure a high salary so their children will then be happy. What they fail to realize is that no salary will ever be enough to make children happy if they do not first understand how to be wise stewards of their resources.

Second, we watched ourselves and the messages from our culture. We observed everything: our habits, our words, television shows, ads, store displays, Christmas traditions, and birthdays. Everything. What messages, subtle or obvious, did we send to the boys about money, possessions, and contentment? Then we modeled and taught. Then we taught and modeled. As parents we knew that we were responsible for the way they saw the world, at least for a little while.

During this time, I remember bringing my children to meet a friend at a bookstore for story hour. This store's marketing strategy was clever—offer parents a free story time and let their children do the rest of the marketing. While I deflected requests from my oldest two for new "really cool" books, my friend's five-year-old son had a different strategy. "Mom, will you put this book on my Christmas list for me?" It was August. My friend had previously explained to her son that she and her husband purchased new books for birthdays and Christmas only. The option of a new book was off his radar, and he accepted that reality. Though my kids saw books as an opportunity to badger Mom, her child saw books as special items that—if worthy—could be added to a Christmas list. Genius.

Not every family we met with was the typical Jones family, living beyond their incomes. Some just sought good counsel. They worked hard to actively build their households on solid financial principles. They knew their expenses, they purposefully saved and gave, and they minimized debt, working toward total elimination of all debts. But it's crucial to look at those who exemplify the Joneses in a general sense and consider the traits they have in common.

If we can study the consistent, underlying issues among these families who ended up in financial ruin, then we can raise our children with an awareness of these truths and set them on a different path. Since our culture tends to look at those who seem to "have it all" with envy and a competitive spirit, we must work purposefully to keep our children and ourselves focused on *not* trying to Keep up with The Joneses.

CHAPTER 3

THE CULTURE OF CONSUMERISM

Families like the Joneses have been around since the days of the early settlers. I'm sure the families from Walnut Grove in the *Little House on the Prairie* series considered the Olsen Family to be the proverbial Jones Family. They had the showy carriage, the fabrics from Europe, and the latest toys for Willie and Nellie. What's unique about our culture now is that families like the lower-income Ingalls can actually come close to keeping up with the Olsens. With easy access to credit and bankers who are willing to let people mortgage a home at 35% of their take-home pay, it's no wonder so many people can actually look like they are "keeping up."

While the concept of using credit (to buy now and pay later) has been around since ancient Egyptian and Babylonian merchants began to accept small payments over time, the idea of easy credit really began to snowball in the early 1980s. Prior to this, individual stores, Diner's Club restaurants, and gas stations all offered their own cards. Only around 1979 when Visa, MasterCard, and American Express become universally accepted and more readily available did the personal credit explosion begin. What better way to stimulate the economy than to give people access to money, so they could buy more of what they want rather than simply what they need?

When credit cards were first offered in the 1950s, the user had to go through a strict screening process before a card would be issued. In the late eighties when my parents dropped me off at college, I had three offers for credit waiting for me in my mailbox and free t-shirts offered if I signed up for a new card at orientation. So as an 18-year-old living on my own for the first time, credit card companies presented me with what sounded like an incredible offer: $500 to use if I needed it, a cool free t-shirt, *and* the opportunity to build my credit score. How could I refuse?

Imagine this situation. An hourly-paid employee receives an offer in the mail for $1,000 to use however he desires. His oldest child needs shoes and his baby needs a car seat. The notion of "easy, low monthly payments" makes it impossible for him to refuse. And so the snowball of debt begins to roll.

Seemingly incredible offers like these tempt young adults and even older adults. Every family we counseled who was facing financial struggles had at least some debt beyond their home and cars. Because debt is now so easy to access and so common to carry, it has become a way of life for many people to see how much they can buy while still managing the minimum payments. It's almost like playing a game.

Newcomers and seasoned veterans alike play the game with similar strategies:

- They secure new credit cards to pay off old cards.
- They borrow money from relatives to buy necessities while using their income to make debt payments.
- They transfer balances to new cards with temporary lower interest rates.
- They take on home equity loans to pay off smaller credit cards.
- They sign up for more new cards to pay the bills after paying the large home equity loan.

The game ends only when they can no longer make their minimum payments and no one else will loan them money. People can play the same game with car payments. For example, Joe Spender likes to buy new cars every few years. He simply rolls his old car debt into the new loan until he realizes he is making a $634 monthly car payment for five years on a car worth $3,000. That's when he calls a financial counselor and admits defeat.

Approximately 40% of Americans admit to living a lifestyle they cannot afford.[1] And those are the ones who know enough to admit it. Consider the impact this has on the American culture. If a large proportion of the population plays this game, then people making average salaries are artificially living at a much higher level than their income really supports. Their friends and neighbors see the new purchases and nice cars and wonder what they're doing wrong to not be able to afford such things. They assume it's not really "fair" that they can't afford a TV or car as nice as someone making the same income, so they too seek out credit and begin to play the game themselves. I'm still waiting for a winner of this game to emerge victorious.

Parents can be the biggest suckers for this game. Who doesn't want to give their child every opportunity available to succeed in the world? What? Piano lessons are $45 an hour? Well, then, we'll just have to "make it work." Travel (or select) soccer is $125 a month plus camps, uniforms, and team spirit wear? OK, we'll figure it out. Often times the "figuring it out" and "making it work" includes using credit cards for so-called emergencies and the regular income for the lessons and camps. The truth is that the "emergencies" should fall into the category of actual expenses that should be planned for— things like a root canal or a new dishwasher. In reality, the lessons and the activity fees are extraneous—they're wants, not needs.

So many parents carry guilt that their houses aren't big enough (no basement or fenced-in yard) or that their kids don't have the latest electronics like "everyone else." But the irony is, when we don't teach our kids to live within their means, we fail to give them the tools they need to become financially solid adults. By giving them the travel team we cannot afford or the lessons we don't have in the budget, we teach them that they deserve to have everything they want and the finances will just work out. They will not succeed financially with this faulty foundation.

Kids learn by watching how their parents use money, and the statistics concerning teens starting college reflect this sobering reality:

- The typical college student receives eight credit card offers their first year.
- Nearly 3 out of 5 students max out their credit cards by the end of freshman year.
- Universities lose more students because of credit card debt than academics.
- The average freshman credit card debt is $1,500.
- Approximately 48% of students make only minimum payments on their credit card bills.
- And 80% don't pay off the card at the end of each month.[2]

Reading these statistics about the behavior of college students might reveal to students that debt doesn't serve them well, prompting them to learn to turn things around financially before they begin living on their own. Unfortunately, that's not the case when you consider these statistics about young adult debt:

- The average young adult has $4,100 in credit card debt.
- Nearly half of young adults have either had a car repossessed, have filed for bankruptcy, or have stopped paying on a debt.
- Twelve million people ages 20-34 live with their parents due to debt.[3]

That final statistic alone should instill fear in every parent. (Not because you don't love your children and would be willing to offer them a roof over their heads during a rough patch, but because you want them to develop into fiscally-responsible adults.)

The easy availability of credit has forever impacted our nation's values concerning money and debt, which influences the culture in which we are raising our children. As we casually stroll the aisles at Best Buy and see the over-sized flat screen TV that our neighbor just bought, we don't have to just dream about it. We don't have to think that we can't afford it. We merely have to consider what freedom in our lives we want to exchange in order to have it.

Social Media Feeds the Beast

Though credit card use has been on the rise for decades, only in recent years has social media like Facebook, Instagram, Pinterest, and Twitter started to impact overconsumption. Television shows and commercials have exposed the nation to how "the other half" lives since the late 1950s, but now people see exactly how their friends and neighbors live, too. They know their friend from high school just got home from a tropical vacation because they see the fabulous pictures. Actually, seven more of their Facebook "friends" also posted pictures from an exotic getaway. "Wait, is everyone going away for spring break?" "Are we the only ones who can't afford to leave the state?" These are dangerous thoughts for families trying to live within their means.

As a result of social media, people have skewed views of the families around them because people post their "Facebook moments" all day long. But those photos offer snapshots of only the best part of life. Vacations. Adorable children. Flowers from husbands. Trophies and certificates. Race winners. It's easy to be convinced that almost everyone married "their best friend and the love of their life," and their life brings nothing but sunshine and roses. People see their friends' children excelling in sports, music, and academia, no doubt the result of extra lessons and coaching.

I remember reading a Facebook post from one of my friends that stated, "Congrats, Shannon, on making that last-second shot to win the tournament. Way to go! Mom and Dad are so proud of you." Can you guess what I thought the following week when my youngest son Matthew had a chance to win his basketball game in the last few seconds, but he missed the shot? Does my son need extra coaching? The same week another post read, "Does anyone in the area know where I can get a good deal on a tux? #sophomoredatingajunior." My son Michael, also a junior, didn't need a tux because he wasn't dating anyone. A parent might reasonably wonder: Is my son not cool enough? When we allow our minds to play the comparison game, we take the focus off our own family and place it on someone else's. Matthew certainly didn't need more coaching—he just missed a shot. And Michael is an amazing young man who will be a great boyfriend, when he is ready.

This daily barrage of everyone's best foot forward certainly can make even a strong person feel insecure and inadequate. I know my dining room table is not set with matching china, placemats, and water goblets. My middle schooler didn't get accepted into National Honor Society. My gourmet dinner is not bubbling in the oven. In an effort to combat or assuage feelings of not measuring up, it becomes easy to start spending money on things that will help us feel like we are just like everyone else. Unfortunately, this tendency to compare and try to keep up often marks the beginning of financial bondage.

We must take these thoughts captive and stop comparing our real lives and our real children with the Facebook lives and children of our friends. I've heard it referred to as Fakebook. Jill Savage, author of *No More Perfect Moms* and *No More Perfect Kids*, confirms, "We must stop comparing our insides to other people's outsides." Unfortunately, some of these posts mask the reality of a family who is living paycheck to paycheck, hoping to make enough minimum payments on credit cards to keep the image intact.

It is quite common for me to visit the house of a young family I'm counseling. These folks, in their late twenties or early thirties, have playrooms that look like Toys "R" Us exploded, nurseries right out of the Pottery Barn catalog, and backyard swing sets more elaborate than the one at the local park. When other young moms visit these homes for a play date, they may leave feeling like they're not doing enough for their child. This leads to discontent, even discouragement. I want to hold their hands and explain to them, "Your children enjoy playing with a box lid and some tape. Your children don't know if their rooms are awesome or not. Your children love to go to the park." Rather than feeling discontent, these moms should realize that by *not* giving their children everything their hearts desire, they are making it easier to raise children who are both content and grateful. By not giving them every material advantage, they are actually giving them a valuable financial advantage for their future.

> *By not giving their children everything their heart's desire, they are making it easier to raise children who are both content and grateful.*

I appreciate a well-appointed nursery, and it certainly doesn't follow that these infants are destined to be materialistic. But it will be more challenging for these parents to instill gratitude in their children for all they have been given, if having the best of everything is all they ever know.

Parents aren't the only ones who become more discontent by using social media. So do kids. As early as elementary school, kids create Instagram accounts and Twitter accounts so they, too, can keep an eye on what their friends are doing, buying, and getting from their parents. A post from a fifth-grade boy simply announced, "These are my new shoes." A close-up picture of two pairs of new Michael Jordan basketball shoes shouted his coolness to the 68 people who "liked" it.

Getting "likes" and "shares" becomes the payment for kids who crave acceptance. Unfortunately, it creates an unhealthy focus on their stuff and how it compares to other kids' stuff. Because a child could potentially follow hundreds of other kids on these sites, any given kid would find it a challenge to keep up with their "friends' " new clothes, shoes, activities, and vacations. But parents can influence their children in a way that will help avoid this competitive madness.

About 75% of the 7th graders in the large middle school where I substitute teach all have Instagram accounts. Yet one free-thinking seventh-grade girl boldly announced she did not. When I asked her why she felt so strongly, she offered the following observations:

> *I saw one of my friends stress out about how she didn't have what everyone else had, that she had to fit in and conform. I tried to explain to her that it was foolish to think this, but she was completely consumed by this one website and the thoughts that were being posted on it. I even witnessed another one of my friends go through serious depression because one of the friends she met on Instagram killed himself. This was over 2 years ago in 2012, and she is still worked up over it. This is only part of the reason why I stay away from social media.*

Few students have the maturity and reasoning capability of this girl. Few students would understand the unhealthy thinking—and even harm—social media can cause.

The Competitive School Environment

Social media is the perfect way to be sure everyone knows what cool stuff a child has or what cool things he's doing. Online competition spills into the school classrooms and hallways. Certainly comparing and measuring up to each other is not a new phenomenon in schools. In the late 1970s, I remember not having as many Bonne Bell Lip Smackers as the other girls in my middle school. Nor did I have an alligator emblem sewn on any of my shirts. My need to fit in was so great that I once cut the alligator emblem off an IZOD shirt my younger brother had gotten from a garage sale, and I awkwardly hand-sewed it onto my own shirt. I can't remember if I fooled anyone, but I clearly remember hearing my mom's shriek from two floors below when she discovered the hole in my brother's new shirt.

Consumer debt was not easy to come by in the 1970s, and I had parents who never would have considered it if it had been, so I survived my middle school years with two Lip Smackers, one fake IZOD shirt my mom let me continue to wear, and an identity that did not revolve around the stuff I had. Of course, having "cool" clothes will not destine your child to a life of financial woes, but do consider how much value you—and your family—assign such things.

These days, very few middle schoolers can navigate the social scene at school without keeping a watchful eye on how their stuff measures up. Boys will usually compare shoes and electronics. Girls often compare clothes, backpacks, and purses. I remember one mother's frantic plight to find just the right $75 Vera Bradley backpack and matching $25 change purse before her sixth-grade daughter began middle school.

Kids start displaying their stuff at school early on. Over two decades ago, I observed a kindergarten class in which a little girl brought in a giant dollhouse for show and tell. The teacher asked if she got it for a birthday present. The girl answered, "No. My mom got it for me because I wanted it." Her fellow students thought the house was "cool" and "awesome," which made the girl herself cool and awesome. And so the cycle began for many of the students in that class who were looking for a little "awesome" themselves.

This problem with using material possessions as a way to measure up is not limited to those families with excessive disposable incomes. Tales from inner-city schools parallel the stories from the suburban schools, only with a slight twist. "The kids have Michael Jordans, but they don't have pencils," explained one teacher from a school in which 75% - 80% of the students ate free or reduced lunches. Despite the lower incomes, most kids in her school carried cell phones—and about half of those were iPhones. "I've worked in the suburban schools, and I've worked here in the city. The only difference is on the specifics of what is valued to spend their money on. Here the girls compete with each other by comparing hair. Some girls easily can spend over $250 on having braids added or on having their own hair braided. These styles must be repeated every couple months to keep it looking up to par. Boys compete by staying current on the latest headphones or the newest Jordan shoes."

No matter where children attend school, whether public or private, inner-city or suburban, large or small, many kids try to make a statement to fellow students about who they are based on the stuff they own. In the past, kids could only compare themselves to other kids at their own school. Now, however, with access to social media, kids can compare themselves to kids across the country 24 hours a day. In their weak and vulnerable moments, preteens and teens log onto their accounts and see what "everyone" else seems to be doing and buying.

This transports them to a dangerous place. Kids can lose themselves for hours, comparing what they have (or don't have) to what other kids have. And by posting photos of their clothes, shoes, electronics, or other possessions, they become part of another teen's angst over what that teen does not have. These kids must understand that behind the smiling faces and the cars with the big bow on the top hides an insecure teen just like themselves. The cheerleader in the UGG boots and the football player with the Dr. Dre headphones are both on a journey to figure out who they are as a person— beyond what they own. If they continue on this path of materialism without a parent to intervene and redirect their focus, they may find themselves on a lifelong quest to find their happiness in their stuff and to find their identity in what they possess.

We are raising children in a culture that values material possessions above character. We are raising children in a culture that makes it easy to use credit cards to buy them almost anything they desire. And we are raising children in a culture where social media publicly displays everyone's possessions and activities for the world to compare. Can we, within our individual families, find a different way? Can we help our kids understand and expose this unhealthy game of comparing and one-upping that too many people play?

Teach your kids to not "play the game." After all, how can you lose a game you're not playing? And why would you want to play a game in which no one wins?

Next Steps

- Talk to your kids about the unhealthy aspects of social media. The pursuit of online popularity can interfere with adolescents discovering their true identity.
- Encourage your kids to not morph into what others want them to be. Talk to them about behaving the same way around friends as they do around family.
- Talk about what is cool and who is cool. Might it be a lot of work to maintain constant cool? Could it be easier to be yourself rather than trying to be someone else's version of cool?
- Empower your kids to make their own unique choices in music, clothing, and activities rather than consuming what the culture feeds them.

CHAPTER 4

THE POWER OF THE FAMILY

In the early 1990s, one of every six children in Philadelphia was born addicted to crack cocaine. In an effort to determine the long-term effects crack addiction would have on the lives of these children, the Philadelphia Child Welfare League conducted a survey of more than 200 babies. All of the babies studied were carried to term and born to impoverished families. Half of the babies weren't exposed to any drugs in utero. Research recorded statistics on these babies for 23 years.

The results shocked everyone involved. After all those years, researchers found no real differences between the babies who were born addicted to crack and those who were not. None. However, they did find something they weren't looking for. They found that children raised in a nurturing home—measured by such factors as warmth, affection and language stimulation—fared far better than kids in a less nurturing home environment. Nurture. Growing up in a nurturing home was a more powerful influence than being addicted to crack cocaine as an infant. [1]

Nurture is defined as caring for someone and encouraging their growth and development. Nurture is powerful. Dr. Robert Brooks, a highly regarded author and speaker on resiliency, asked this question, "Why do some children who grow up in poverty and racism, undergo trauma, or face some other kind of adversity do well while others don't?" His thorough research found that those kids who broke out of the cycle of poverty or adversity had one significant trait in common: They had an encouraging adult in their life. Someone who believed in them. Someone who nurtured their spirit.[2]

Christine Carter, PhD and author of *Raising Happiness,* concurs with this wisdom:

> *Turns out that there are two things that influence how materialistic kids are. The first is obvious: Consciously or not, we adults socialize kids to be materialistic. When parents—as well as peers and celebrities—model materialism, kids care more about wealth and luxury. So when parents are materialistic, kids are likely to follow suit. Same thing with television viewing: The more TV kids watch, the more likely they are to be materialistic.*
>
> *The less obvious factor behind materialism has to do with the degree to which our needs are being filled. When people feel insecure or unfulfilled—because of poverty or because a basic psychological need like safety, competence, connectedness, or autonomy isn't being met—they often try to quell their insecurity by striving for wealth and a lot of fancy stuff. Because of this, relatively poor teenagers ironically tend to be more materialistic than wealthy ones. And less nurturing and more emotionally cold mothers tend to have more materialistic offspring.*[3]

A nurturing parent has the power to fill the psychological needs of competence and connectedness. They have the power to model confidence and security apart from what they possess. Nurturing parents can create an environment in the home where children can grow into healthy adults who are not negatively impacted by our culture of materialism.

All four of my sons have always attended public schools. Given that the schools they attend are relatively large and quite affluent, friends have asked me if they struggle with the socially competitive environment. Do they have trouble trying to keep up with their peers and their possessions? Is it difficult in such a sexualized environment? Is there a lot of pressure on them concerning college acceptance?

While all those concerns are present at theirs and almost every school in our nation, my sons have not been impacted in a detrimental way. They are certainly not problem-free, but their challenges have not resulted from cultural influences. I like to think of the metaphor of a sponge. If I place a dry sponge in a small bowl of vinegar, it will quickly absorb most of the vinegar in the bowl. But if I first soak that sponge in water and then place it into the bowl of vinegar, it absorbs very little vinegar. As parents, we can "fill up our kids" with so much love, perspective, and wisdom, that when they navigate the culture at large, it does not impact them as much. If we intentionally pour into our children our insights and values, they will be better prepared to respond to the world's alternative offers.

Connect Well with Each Child

Passing on our wisdom and values to our kids is not possible until we have first connected with them. We must be someone who is important to them, and they must know how important they are to us. Connecting well means each of your children should *feel* unconditionally loved, so that, no matter what they do, they know you can't love them any more. No matter what awards they win, what sports they excel at, or what grades they earn, they know you cannot love them more than you already do. It also means that no matter what they do, they know you can't love them any less (even those who deliberately rebel in an effort to make you love them less).

Despite poor choices, temper tantrums, and rude behavior, you will love them with a full heart. Part of feeling loved is being known and feeling cherished for who the child is at their core. Knowing them and loving them, tantrums and all, is what connects us deeply with our children.

Part of knowing them deeply is recognizing how God specifically designed each one. I remember how Charles Boyd's book, *Different Children, Different Needs*, forever altered the way I parented my boys. For the first time, I realized each of them had traits that were hard-wired into them. These were traits I couldn't change despite the fact that I sometimes

> *Knowing them and loving them, tantrums and all, is what connects us deeply with our children.*

wished Michael was less opinionated and Bryan was more outgoing. I sometimes *wished* Matthew was calmer and Christopher was less particular. The following is a list of a few of the many traits that could have driven me crazy, until I realized these were a part of who each of my children was designed to be:

- high energy
- low energy
- likes routine—needs routine—changes in routines bring stress
- hates routines—likes being spontaneous
- flexible and easy going
- determined and convicted
- particular
- carefree
- social and outgoing
- needs time alone
- finds school to be easy
- finds school to be challenging
- competitive and aggressive
- likes the limelight

- hates the limelight
- makes decisions quickly
- needs lots of information before making a decision

How can understanding your child's hard-wiring help you parent more effectively? Once I understood that Bryan needed routines and predictability to feel secure, I was more careful to prepare him for upcoming changes in our schedule. When I understood that Matthew had more energy than the other boys, I found healthy ways for him to expend any extra energy. I gave slow-paced Christopher more time to get ready in the morning while Michael could be ready and out the door ten minutes after I woke him. When you begin working with their temperaments rather than against them, parenting becomes much easier.

Not only do we connect better with our kids when we know them intimately, but we can also teach them about who they are and how they were designed. Point out that things that are easy for them might not be so easy for other kids, and vice-versa. Read studies and books about personalities and talk about how God uniquely designed them. I have been teaching at the middle school level for over 25 years, observing thousands of kids trying to figure out who they are apart from their parents. This journey is so much easier for those kids who have a clear sense of their strengths and weaknesses as well as a confidence that they are deeply loved for exactly who they are.

One of the easiest ways to deepen your relationship with each of your children is to spend time alone with them. Easier said than done, I know. Sometimes my alone time with one of my kids was talking while we folded laundry or walked the dog together. This time enabled me to value each child as an individual rather than one of the group. When our sons were all under age six, I felt as though I would never be alone again. They literally clung to me or followed me around the house. But even in all that togetherness, if I didn't take a few minutes to purposefully connect, days could go by where life just happened without ever relating at the heart level. As they have grown, the boys have spent long hours away from our home, either in school, at friend's houses, or at work, but our connection remains strong. Hugs, pats on the back, foot rubs, or chats on the back porch all work to solidify this relationship between us.

To confess, I rarely played games with my boys when they were little. I didn't really enjoy it. The games seemed to go on forever, the cherries kept tipping out of the Hi Ho Cherry-O bucket, and I couldn't make my super hero do the right things. "Mom, that guy doesn't do that. That's not his weapon. You're not doing it right." Rather than games, I found other ways to stay close emotionally, and my sons learned to play for hours—together or separate—without adult supervision. What's critical is recognizing the power in intentionally developing a deep relationship with each of your children. It's worth taking the time in order to avoid the potential struggles that can occur when a child feels disconnected from his family. This preventative work is no different than taking the time to caulk a crack in the foundation of your home so that water doesn't seep in later and cause the whole wall to crumble.

Connect as a Family

Connecting as a family is just as important as connecting with your kids individually. I love hearing stories about how families connect with each other because the stories are as unique as the families who tell me. Consider how your family chooses to relate to each other. What are your traditions and rituals? What special places do you enjoy frequenting? What inside jokes would others never understand?

Traditions

One of the most important parts of being a mom is creating a safe and nurturing environment where the family wants to spend time. I try to think of our home as a sanctuary. School is a tough place for a couple of my boys. Long days, challenging studies, and (sometimes) mean people can tend to overwhelm them. But when the boys come home, they feel loved and supported for who they are. The pace slows. They feel a part of something. One way to create this family unity and bonding is through rituals and traditions. It's important to realize that I am not talking about Pinterest-worthy rituals where we bedazzle matching t-shirts before our outing to the zoo; we actually don't even have to try very hard for something to become a tradition.

I remember one Christmas after we decorated the tree the boys asked, "Are we going to sleep under the Christmas tree tonight?" What? We had done that only one year, but clearly it meant something to them. So, since it appeared it was now a tradition, I let them all get their sleeping bags and curl up under the glowing tree—even though it was a school night. Traditions simply evolve. A friend of mine buys a new board game every time they take a vacation, and the family plays the game every night during the trip. She, too, started that "tradition" after her children asked, "What game are we going to take on our trip this year?" For a mere $10.00, they birthed a tradition, created new memories, and solidified family bonds.

Family meetings, game nights, cleaning parties, camping, 18-hour car trips, yard work days, a half-gallon of ice cream and six spoons, carnivals in the basement, and playing poker with Jolly Ranchers are just part of what it means to grow up as a Miller. Each of these activities took on lives of their own after we did them once or twice. Because they resonated with our family, we kept doing them. Because we kept doing them, they became part of our identity. With time, your family will develop its own identity. By observing your own unique design, you can give your kids a sense of membership into something bigger than themselves. Ask them what they like most about being a part of the family. What do they like least? Even camping in the rain or shoveling mulch all day became memories that served to bind our family together. With our unique traditions and rituals in place, it's easy to instruct our boys, "You're a Miller, and Millers try to always…"

One of our favorite traditions when the boys were younger was having Boys Day Out. This gave my husband the chance to have the kids all on his own, while offering me a monthly respite. The boys planned the entire day. It usually included a park, some ice cream, and quite often a trip to "The Indian Reservation." My husband simply ran out of things to do with them one day and needed to kill a little more time, so he parked the car at a large corn field bordered by a small wooded area. He intended to take them on a walk in the woods not far from our home. "What's this place?" they asked him.

"This? You want to know what *this* is? Well . . . this is . . . an ancient Indian reservation . . . " And so the tale began. The tale lasted seven years and included such highlights as finding "arrowheads" (triangle shaped stones), ancient "pottery" (field debris), and even a "stagecoach hitch" (a rusted John Deer tractor part). But after a few years, my husband felt like he needed to spice things up, so he ordered actual Native American artifacts from a reservation in Arizona and hid them in the woods and field. On the next trip to The Reservation, they decided to dig around for buried artifacts. Amazingly they found four bear claw necklaces and some real Native American arrows. Miraculously, a real bow still hung in a tree. This tradition became so rooted in our family's culture that even on Michael's 14th birthday, he wanted to celebrate by looking around The Reservation. Traditions connect families.

Rites of Passage

Rites of passage offer another opportunity for families to build community with each other. Cultures all over the world have unique celebrations to mark the passage into adulthood. These rituals bond the community together, even among generations. At our house, we have special celebrations that honor specific ages:

- 5—not a little kid any more
- 10—double digits
- 13—teenager
- 16—driving and dating (in theory)
- 18—an adult

These are not elaborate events. Instead, they encompass something simple, like hiking alone with Dad in the back woods, planning and taking an overnight trip anywhere in the state, or receiving a special knife. These rites of passage create structure in the family and give kids an added sense of belonging to something with routines, rituals and celebrations. Street gangs flourish where families have given up their influence, yet the kids still yearn for a place to belong. Stories are frequently told about painful initiation rites for gang members, but kids are willing to endure these awful rites in order to find community and belonging

We must become our children's "gang," the group with which they primarily identify. We must make our homes the hangout—a safe place where they feel known and accepted. We must have our own rituals and rites of passage to help them feel a part of something bigger than themselves.

Vacations and Special Places

Ask any adult about their special memories from childhood, and they will almost always include vacations. Please take this to heart: A vacation does not need to be expensive in order to be memorable. Our culture can make parents feel like a trip to Disney World is a rite of passage for every child—it is not. After my five-year-old nephew caught his first fish at our house one summer, he announced, "Dad, this is better than Disney!" I'm sure my brother wasn't thrilled to hear that newsflash after spending thousands of dollars at The Magic Kingdom just two months before.

When my boys were younger, Andy and I spent quite a few summers camping for a week near the ocean on Cape Cod for less than the cost of a single day at an all-inclusive resort. Going back to the same place for a number of years also provides for memories to cover the passage of time. The boys remember being afraid of the waves when they were toddlers, and they remember riding on jet skis when they were older. Returning to the same place also allows for those nostalgic conversations about prior trips: "Remember that one time when we found the stray cat and you tried to sneak it into the camper?" These stories of adventures away from home become the fabric that keeps the family knitted together.

Actually families don't even need to leave home to get the vacation feel. In recent years, "staycations" have become popular. The routine changes and rather than leaving home, the family simply lives as if they are on vacation. Kids can brainstorm places to visit each day. Board games and long walks replace television and computer time. The focus shifts to relaxing and enjoying each other rather than the busyness of life.

Families can also simply have special places. Psychologist Mary Pipher, author of *The Shelter of Each Other*, writes, "Places can protect families as well. Families can have their spots—particular restaurants, parks, museums, front porches or street corners—where they like to be together. These sacred places can be anywhere— kitchens, ball fields, state parks or bowling alleys. I may be biased in my thinking that the best spots are in natural settings. One of the greatest gifts parents can give their children is to teach them to love the natural world." [4] Pipher understands the impact of spending time with our families enjoying nature.

For some reason people feel like their greatest gift to their children is the biggest house they can afford. But children actually prefer small spaces, such as tree houses, alleys, secret rooms, and crawl spaces under stairways. When we moved to a larger house that had a basement, the boys refused to go down there without me for over a year. They preferred our smaller house where they could always hear my voice no matter what room they were in.

Family Meals

Numerous studies reinforce the importance of families eating meals together. One in particular by Dr. Catherine Snow at Harvard's Graduate School of Education, followed 65 families over 15 years, looking at how mealtime conversations play a critical role in language acquisition in young children.[5] The conversations that occur around the family table teach children more vocabulary than they learn when you read to them. Improved vocabularies help kids become better readers. Better readers do better in all school subjects.

Miriam Weinstein dedicates her entire book, *The Surprising Power of Family Meals: How Eating Together Makes Us Smarter, Stronger, Healthier, and Happier*, to the simple concept that eating meals together as a family is important and benefits the child in a variety of areas.[6]

A *Reader's Digest* survey of more than 2,000 high-school seniors compared academic achievement with family characteristics. The study indicated that eating meals with the family was a stronger predictor of academic success in children than whether they lived with one or both parents.[7] Share that research with families who may not have much money or education or a two-parent household but do have it in their power to eat with their kids!

In another research project coordinated by Dr. Blake Bowden of Cincinnati Children's Hospital, researchers studied 527 teenagers to determine what family and lifestyle characteristics influenced good mental health and adjustment. He found that kids who ate dinner with their families at least five times per week were the least likely to take drugs, feel depressed or get into trouble.[8]

So that "five mandatory meals" are not added to your already stress-riddled to-do list, let me again confess that our family dinner count is sometimes only two meals a week with everyone present. I want to have beautiful family dinners, but life happens. Teenagers work and have sports. Middle schoolers have band performances and piano lessons. Parents have church meetings and date nights. I think what these studies really point to is this: children have an easier time growing up when they live in families who cherish one another, talk to one another, and feel connected to one another.

Knowing our kids, understanding how they are designed, and spending time with them allows us to create a nurturing environment where kids can mature in a healthy way. A nurturing family whose members are committed to each other is a powerful defense against the culture of materialism and consumerism.

CHAPTER 5

FIGHTING FOR INFLUENCE

Every child has a family, but not every family has a powerful influence on the child. Some families lose the battle for their children's allegiance. If we fail to connect our children to the family or if we allow mass media to overstep its boundaries, we lose our influence—the same influence that, only a few generations ago, nearly every family had without even trying.

> *If we allow mass media to overstep its boundaries, we lose our influence.*

Despite the fact that American parents are raising their children in a generally materialistic culture—especially when compared with the rest of the world, we have the power within our families to create a different culture at home, one that's significantly stronger than the one outside.

Last summer, as I drove down the road with my two teenage boys in the car, I noticed two middle school girls walking down the street in tiny shorts and tiny tank tops. I didn't say a word, but one of the boys said, "Wow, that's sad." Rather than seeing two "hot girls" they could ogle, they saw two girls, someone's daughters and sisters, who presented their bodies to the world for strangers to gawk at. I smiled as I realized my husband and I had won that battle—successfully negating the culture's message about hot girls. (Note: We don't always win those battles or those that relate to selfishness, pride, annoying habits, personal grooming, tempers, tidiness, money or a million other issues teenagers deal with. Like you, we continually strive to lay the foundation, instill godly values and leave the rest up to the Lord. But we won that day, and I celebrated inwardly.)

The reason my sons view their world this way is because we have spoken out against referring to girls as "hot." From the time they were in grade school, we pounded this message into them. We have taught them that girls are special and need to be treated differently than boys. (Not a politically correct message but one we feel will help them learn to honor their wives someday.) When they used to make "farting noises" with their armpits or talk about bodily functions, we told them not to do those things around girls or grown-ups. We've talked about our culture and how it often objectifies women. We've talked about the importance of modesty and purity. Conversations about their future wives have always been so commonplace that I remember one of them getting upset with his brother and shouting, "When you grow up, you'll never get anyone to be your wife!"

Addressing which pop-culture messages disagree with our messages is key. When we watched Adam Sandler's movie *Grown Ups* together, I paused the disc on one scene in particular. "Look, guys. See what is happening? See what the movie director is trying to teach?" A "hot," twenty-something girl had lifted up the hood of an old car trying to determine what was wrong with it. She tilted her head back, her face in a pout. At the same time, steam released from the engine and blew upward toward her face. In slow motion, her white blouse blew open in the wind as music played. Immediately, the camera shifted to the faces of two 12-year-old boys observing the girl. Their mouths were dropped open and their eyes were wide. Our culture often teaches boys to view girls sexually, as objects of physical desire. Culture also teaches girls that this is the best way to get boys' attention. By training our own children to develop an awareness of how culture is transferred, we can help them decipher truth from propaganda.

Television—the First Battleground

Since the popularity of television began in the 1950s, families have had to fight for the influence they once held innately for centuries. Throughout history, culture has been passed from generation to generation vertically, from the parents and other adults in the community to the children. But with the popularity of television and the increase of peer influence, culture is frequently passed horizontally—child to child, student to student, athlete to athlete. We see evidence of this any time kids end up talking like each other, dressing like each other, and looking to each other for how to behave.

Some parents leave children unattended watching TV for hours. These same well-meaning moms and dads, hurried and harried by life, would never allow a stranger to tell their kids that their parents are losers or that hurting people is a great way to solve problems. Yet these are the messages the people on television whisper to our kids everyday. By ignoring what our kids are watching on TV, we make it difficult to keep our own values at the forefront.

Don't be afraid to place limits on TV, but don't make it the forbidden fruit, either. The notion of taboo tends to spark an even greater interest in something. Monitor TV watching and set clear boundaries, but more importantly, get your kids outside and moving. Ideally, kids will have other hobbies and interests and not really have much use for watching TV or movies. They will realize that life (real, vibrant life) happens apart from the glowing box.

The content of television has changed significantly over the years. Rather than Beaver and Mrs. Cleaver and Carol Brady and the Brady Bunch, television shows feature siblings who routinely argue and barely tolerate each other at best. Parents and most adults are portrayed as totally out of touch, disconnected, and weird. Only the kids are cool. The Disney Channel is a popular culprit that creates shows in which the vast majority of kids are wealthy with an incredible eye for fashion and fun. In a word, they rule! These young TV kids often speak rudely and harshly to their parents. Then, when they become teens, they yearn to get away from their parents completely. The 8th grade son of a friend of mine said to his mom, "I don't get it. Am I supposed to hate you for some reason?" This boy still enjoyed hanging out with his mom, yet messages from friends and television indicated this was abnormal behavior.

According to Psychologist Mary Pipher, "We are a culture that portrays parents as baggage, impossible to ignore but generally a pain in the neck. Teenagers hear that families are a hindrance to individual growth and development, and sadly, teens who love their parents are made to feel odd. This sets teenagers up for trouble. Just when teenagers desperately need their parents' guidance and support, they are culturally conditioned to break away." [1]

Kids need their parents to help them mature in a healthy way. Their fellow teens do not have the wisdom or unconditional love to help them grow. Parents alone have those things teens so desperately need.

Gloria DeGaetano, author of *Parenting Well in a Media Age*, speaks out harshly against the toxic nature of the culture at large. "Ideally, we'd live in a larger culture that affirms the morals, values, and attitudes, and behaviors we teach our children, a culture that affirms our parental voice. But we don't." She refers to it as an "industry-generated" culture in which the large corporations and media giants influence many aspects of our lives with their own agendas. It is not only the messages of teen rebellion and angst that hurt children, but also the message that a company's product will fill a void by making a child feel alive, independent, valuable, and grown-up. [2]

The Isolating Impact of Texting

Moreover, in recent years, the outside culture has bombarded our homes with the increased popularity of texting. The industry-generated culture is first transferred to those kids with TVs in their rooms and no limits on their screen time. Then those kids pass it along to their more sheltered friends. With texting, a teen can literally have conversations with their friends all night long. Frequently, teens place their cell phones by their heads at night in case texts come in. (Because teen friendships are insecure by nature, a missed text might send the wrong message that the relationship wasn't important enough to respond.)

Consider this irony: Because kids who have already disconnected from their families feel an intense need to stay connected with someone, they find other ways to fill that void, often connecting incessantly with friends via texts. Cell phones further disconnect families because often there is no longer a house phone to monitor who is calling and how often. Children retreat to their rooms—or other places apart from the rest of the family—to talk and text. They connect with their peers in isolation from parents, and their connection to the culture at large continues its insidious growth.

When I was growing up and a friend called our house, my dad would talk to them for a few minutes before he even handed me the phone. He knew who my friends were, and he connected with them when they called. With texting, kids don't even have to come to the door to pick up their friends. They simply text "here" to signal their arrival. Studies show clearly that children who pursue higher levels of media involvement (TV, magazines, Internet) are much more likely to abuse drugs and alcohol or suffer from depression and anxiety.[3] Perhaps it is the pulling away from family that removes the safety net of their nurturing environment and starts them on the path to self-medicating with drugs and alcohol.

But we do not need to passively sit back and lose our power. Parents can certainly set limits on phone use, but more importantly, they can talk about its dangers. Parents of girls more often witness the harsh reality of cruel texts, forwarded messages from frenemies, and screen shots posted to Instagram for the world to judge. Talk to teens. Tell them how difficult it is to grow up under a spotlight of potential social judgment.

One 8th grade girl told her friends that her mom was to blame for keeping her off Instagram and for taking texting off her phone, but the reality was they decided this together. The girl felt emotionally safer without friends and non-friends having access to her 24-hours a day, and her mom was more than happy to be the "bad guy" in this decision and accept the blame. If parents initiate these discussions well before the middle school years, they'll already have a foundation in place when issues surrounding social media begin.

Reflect back to your own middle school days. Do you remember going home and finally getting away from the drama at school? What if that drama followed you home and announced itself every three minutes with a muffled *beep*? What if you had nowhere to go to find peace and rest?

The Explosion of Kids' Activities

Recent decades have also seen the transformation of kids' activities. Some maintain that skyrocketing college tuition costs have prompted parents to focus more intently on the possibility of sports or academic scholarships. Or maybe activities have increased simply because there are more available now. No one played travel (or select) sports when I grew up in the 1970s because no popular travel sports programs existed. Schools had teams. Towns had leagues for sports in a specific season. But despite how much my brother loved playing basketball, he could play only from October to February on a team. These days, my youngest son plays on a basketball team ten months a year. And it's not even one that "travels."

Busyness resulting from over-involvement in activities can rob families of true connecting time because it has a tendency to kick up the stress level in the house. Shuttling kids to activities might seem like time well spent together. More often, if the parent acts merely as a chauffeur, then the family has not truly connected. Quality time requires discipline and intentionality to make it work. I know one mom who purposefully uses carpool time to connect with her tween son about his thoughts and feelings. She says her son is better able to communicate about the deeper issues because he sits in the back seat and can't see her face. She has also designated her car to be an "electronics free zone," which makes conversations easier and more meaningful.

What about spending time together as your child's coach? Even parents who coach their child's team must remember there is a difference between directing your son's baseball practice and playing catch with him in the yard. The backyard relationship is about the joy of being together and sharing an interest, whereas coaching can, at times, feel more performance-based to the child. Plus, a coach must divide his time among all the players; he can't give his son or daughter the one-on-one attention they crave and need.

No matter what causes the increased busyness, parents have the power to monitor and amend the family's schedule in order to leave room for ample opportunities to simply relax and enjoy each other's presence. A middle school girl once wrote in her journal at school, "My mom's there when I need her, and she's there when I don't." The media blitz about quality time has caused some parents to forget that it's this simple power of our presence that also helps kids feel loved and secure.

It would be ironic if "add more free time" became a burden on your to-do list. But purposefully creating margins in your schedule will keep the pace less hectic and the climate more peaceful. Ann Kroeker, author *of Not So Fast—Slow Down Solutions for Frenzied Families,* explains, "We're raising our kids in a high-speed, high pressured, 24/7 world. Pushing children to get ahead, we cram everything possible into our days to maximize their chance at success. We're overloaded, overextended, and over-caffeinated. And we're paying a price."[4] She inspires families to make simple changes to reclaim time to rest and to enjoy one another.

Advertising Ploys

When we manage the influence of television, texting, and activities, we have an impact with our kids that other parents have forfeited. When parents give up their influence, materialism grows in our families, because the culture tells them who they are. When they question "Who am I?" as all kids do, the reply is "You are what you do. You are what you have. You are what you look like." However, children who are connected to their parents and have a more accurate picture of themselves will be much less likely to be influenced by our culture.

For decades, advertising ploys have tried to entice children to find their identity in their stuff. According to Nancy Shalek, president of the Shalek Agency, "Advertising at its best is making people feel that without their product, you're a loser. Kids are very sensitive to that . . . You open up emotional vulnerabilities, and it's very easy to do with kids because they are most emotionally vulnerable." [5] Ad agencies strategically target the emotional vulnerabilities of kids.

Ads try to develop an association between the product and the child's very identity. As you watch commercials, notice how many ads for kids present children with other children having a great time—lots of well-dressed children smiling and laughing. Clearly the advertised product appears to bring more popularity. And popularity is fun. If children are insecure in their identities or lack confidence in their inherent value, the company's product might be just what they need to feel secure.

This is the ad agency's strategy, but we have the power to stage a counter-attack. We can stop surrendering our power to the culture. We can start maximizing the influence we have with our kids by knowing them, spending time with them, and teaching them who they are. And we can nurture their spirit so their need for security and significance is already met.

CHAPTER 6

THE GIFT OF ENOUGH

The Johnson family had saved for years to take their children to Disney World. Yet despite being in the place "where all your dreams come true," three-year-old Katie was soon distraught. She had just seen a large pink balloon with Mickey Mouse ears tucked inside, and she wanted one. Immediately. When her dad said, "No," the tears began to fall. When the tears didn't change his mind, she opted for the mini-fit. When that proved fruitless, she attempted the full-blown temper tantrum. At last, Dad finally realized the balloon was really important to her and bought her one. Problem solved.

Actually, a new problem began that day—one that might be financially devastating for Katie and her own family one day. Katie didn't understand the concept of Enough. She was in the middle of the place where all her dreams were supposed to come true, and instead she was focused on what she still did not have—a latex balloon with Mickey Mouse ears inside. The truth is, until Katie understood how much is Enough, she would never be able to have all her dreams come true.

In order for kids, even as young as Katie, to understand the concept of Enough, they must recognize the continuum of:

SCARCITY—ENOUGH—ABUNDANCE—TOO MUCH

The mistake that many parents like Katie's make is that they want to give their kids abundance. (Think Christmas morning surprises, birthday presents stacked high, and extravagant vacations.) But they have never taught their kids how much is Enough. If we fail to teach Enough, then how can a child ever appreciate abundance?

Teaching "Enough"

Use the continuum above and a large bag of M&Ms to teach kids this concept. Write out the word *scarcity* on an index card and then place no candies on that card. Then write out the word *enough* on the next card and place a small pile of M&Ms on that card. Write the word *abundance* on the third card and place a good size pile on the card. Finally, pour the rest of the bag on the final index card and mark it *too much*. Sure, a few kids will argue that that is not too much, but they will get the idea.

Ask them which pile looks like the amount most kids would like to eat at one time. Have them explain why. Ask if they would be grateful to receive this amount of M&Ms. Ask them why. Take a look at the pile labeled "too much." What might happen if a kid did eat it all? Too much is never good for the person with too much. It harms them. Have kids brainstorm how too much of something can be harmful (too much sun, too much medicine, too much pop).

Now, tell them that the problem is that many kids do not understand how much is enough, so when they receive abundance they simply think that it is enough, and they are not overly excited about it or grateful for it.

You can also give them a few scenarios to help apply this concept. Have them imagine that they were sitting in church listening to the sermon quietly and their dad leaned over and gave them two M&Ms. How would they feel? Because they were expecting no treats during church, two M&Ms would feel like abundance. They would be excited because it was enough to just sit and listen in church; they expected nothing. Two small M&Ms were as exciting as a giant pile in the demonstration above. Our expectations in situations impact our happiness.

Once your kids are school-age you can ask them why they think some kids do not appreciate all that they have. Ask if there are kids at their school who seem to have a lot of stuff. Are the kids at school who have "everything" content with what they have or do they want even more? Do these kids talk about the stuff they still are planning to get? So even though these kids have a lot of stuff, they still want more and more? Why do you think that is?

Guide your kids to the basic idea that if kids do not have an awareness of how much is enough, then they will constantly seek more. You can take it one step further for older kids and talk about the problem with gaining your identity through the things that you have rather than the person that you are inside and your position as a child of God.

> *If kids do not have an awareness of how much is enough, then they will constantly seek more.*

Another way to teach Enough is to regularly use the word *enough* with your kids. Use it daily. In order for them to become familiar with the concept, they have to hear the word often and in a variety of situations.

"You have had enough juice already."

"You have enough stuffed animals."

"One scoop of ice cream is enough."

"Eating out twice a month is enough."

"You already have enough of those."

"$5 is enough to spend for that. We are not spending $8."

"You have played with that long enough."

"You have spent enough time with friends."

By hearing the word frequently, kids will quickly learn to distinguish between enough and more than enough. They will begin to apply the filter of Enough for themselves. They will think, "I have enough mechanical pencils already, but this one is really cool." "I already ate enough M&M's for one day so I'd better keep the rest for later." "I spent enough money at the mall for today, so I will save the rest." Encouraging kids to create their own filter of Enough empowers them to be able to see the financial and even non-financial decisions that they make in terms of this plumb line of Enough.

The Danger of Comparisons

One of the problems with helping our children understand the concept of Enough is that many of their classmates are living with abundance every day. These are the kids who order stacks of books each month from the Scholastic book order. They see all the cool movies the weekend they come out. They wear the latest fashions and buy the latest electronics within days of their release date. They collect basketball shoes in the same way other kids collect basketball cards. They bring $20 to the annual book fair and buy an extra ice cream bar at lunch every day.

These luxuries aren't treats for them. Because they are everyday occurrences, these experiences are simply part of their version of enough. Rarely are these kids grateful for these luxuries because the experiences have become a natural part of their day.

My own sons are not usually grateful for the air conditioning in our home—until it breaks down. It is during these times of scarcity, when Mom has to wipe their backs and foreheads with a cool cloth before bed, that they learn to be grateful for air conditioning. Much of the world has no running water in their homes, yet we fill glass after glass without a thought. Rather than remembering those who have less, we tend to compare ourselves with others who have more, thus robbing us and our children of the opportunity to be grateful.

Because having water or air conditioning does not bring our family joy on a daily basis, I can use this concept to talk to my kids about the gratitude they feel and the joy they experience when we do something special. If something is commonplace, it's challenging to remember that we should be grateful for it. It's challenging to be joyful about it.

As a family, however, we can fight the culture of excess so that we can experience gratitude and joy for what we are blessed to have. We are not going to buy books from the book order every month because we don't need them, and we would no longer be excited on those occasions when we saved up and bought a special book. We are not going to buy treats at lunch every day so that the ice cream we buy on Fridays will be a source of excitement.

This is a concept that kids can understand. They can see with their own eyes that the kids who already have so much usually want more. Rather than being jealous of the boy who got to spend $100 on spirit wear at school orientation, they can use it as an opportunity to be grateful for the clothes they do have and do take for granted. They can find something in the spirit wear shop that they really love and put it on a Christmas or birthday list. Or they can look at the spirit wear and realize that they really wouldn't be that excited about anything after a few weeks anyway. By understanding the concept of Enough, kids can become very skilled at looking at a purchase and seeing it beyond the first week of ownership.

Because my four boys have been savvy to this concept since they were toddlers, they have, at times, surprised a few people with their life-view. When my third son, Christopher, was in kindergarten, his teacher shared with us her observation that he had refused to fill out his "wish list" for the school's book fair that week. Apparently, each class was taken down to the book fair in the library so the kids could shop for books. Each student was asked to write the names of all the books (and other goodies like scented erasers and invisible-ink pens) they wanted on a list and then bring these lists home. The parents would see the list and send money to school for the child to buy the books at the end of the week. Simple.

According to the teacher, Christopher said he didn't need to fill out the list. When the teacher asked him why he didn't need to, he stated matter-of-factly, "I already have enough books and these aren't really a good deal anyway."

Lest you think I celebrated my supreme counter-culture victory, two years later Matthew was in kindergarten. His book fair list was sent home—he had written on every line on the front and then he added lines on the back! We spent some time looking through the list carefully and talking about which *one* book out of them all might be the very best one. Though this was a challenging task, he finally selected *Bad Kitty Takes a Bath*. Yes, this book was the best of the best. This would be the treasured book. I snuck over to school that week and bought the book. Rather than giving it to him, I hid it in my closet for his Easter basket a mere four weeks later. (Yes, this made him the kid who didn't buy a book at the book fair, but he didn't really mind at all.)

But when Easter morning came (video camera poised to capture forever the thrill of the surprise) Matthew tore open the wrapping paper, looked at the book, looked at me and said, "Cool! Thanks! A book." Then he put it down and grabbed another present. I'm not sure if he even remembered wanting it. That seems to be the reality of most of what our kids want—it starts with a high-intensity ask, but then the allure fades.

G.K. Chesterton explained it this way, "There are two ways to get enough—one is to continue to accumulate more and more; the other is to desire less." Many families attempt to acquire Enough by accumulating more and more. The latest fashions, newly released electronics, and must-see vacations can lead them on the road to financial disaster before they ever realize that they already had achieved Enough.

When Michael was six, he found a little plastic Snoopy guy that looked interesting to him. He loved Snoopy. He also loved whacking tennis balls at the garage door. *This* Snoopy was actually holding a tennis racquet. Immediately cool—and Michael had enough money saved to buy him. But as he was looking at it, his little brother Bryan chimed in, "I wouldn't get it. It's just going to end up at the bottom of the toy tub!" Brilliant. Bryan was able to forecast into the future and realize that the odds of this being a treasured item were slim. Snoopy was likely to be played with for a week or two and then banished to the bottom of the plastic tub of toys in the basement. Michael considered this wisdom and left Snoopy at the store. He had enough toys like this one.

As parents, we must realize that we are not depriving our children when we do not buy them what they ask for. Is the mom who says "No" to cookies for breakfast or chocolate milk in their cereal depriving her children? In the same way, we are not depriving our children of abundance and happiness

> *We must realize that we are not depriving our children when we do not buy them what they ask for.*

when we take the time to ensure that they understand how much is Enough. Because the reality is, there will always be someone who has more, stores that offer more, and television shows that depict more. As the saying goes—we cannot prepare the road for the child; instead we must prepare the child for the road. Our kids need to navigate the materialistic culture they are living in. But it wasn't always like it is now.

Back in the Day

I love to hear stories from older people who grew up before this age of materialism took root. I love hearing about the simplicity of their childhoods and the sweet nostalgia of being young, joyful, and carefree. My teaching experiences have introduced me to so many kids who lacked the innocent joy of childhood that once seemed to be a given. Instead, many kids living in our culture are now preoccupied with what others have, what they want to have, and what they have that others don't have. Rather than experiencing joy and simplicity, they are frustrated, anxious, and continually seeking more.

I spoke with one man from my church who is in his early 90's about his childhood memories from the Great Depression. I was so enamored with this vision of yesteryear that I asked him to write about it for me. I asked him to include what he thought the differences were with kids today. Even in his writing I can feel the joy of his simple childhood come through in his words and punctuation.

> *I was born and raised on a farm. I helped raise the chickens and gather eggs. These were "chores" but also lots of fun! I learned a lot about "life" from watching the animals on the farm. =)*
>
> *My dad made toys for us. We had a homemade swing, slide and a merry-go-round. My bike was made from parts discarded from other bikes and then welded together. We played with bottle caps (caps off of soda bottles) and used them to make roads, buildings and houses. The only toys that we had that were purchased were a few 10-cent cars, sidewalk skates that we bought used, and an old red wagon. We didn't have much, but the little we did have provided hours and hours of fun! We were very happy!*
>
> *The children in my neighborhood were all equally poor, but none of us knew we were poor. We got along well together for the most part and entertained ourselves hour by hour. There were about 20-25 neighborhood kids and we all played together under the streetlights until our parents called us in.*
>
> *Kids today seem to spend a lot of alone time on the computer or with hand held devices, phones, etc. They don't spend as much time communicating because they can pretty much entertain themselves. As a child, the kids entertained themselves by doing things together and playing together.*
>
> *I do not think kids are happier today just because they have a lot of "things" to entertain themselves. My*

*childhood was extremely happy and I wouldn't change
it for anything!*

*I grew up with limited "stuff". Yes, I had a few toys,
but most of the time "playtime" involved the use of my
imagination. I (and my friends my age) saved things to
play with...used cardboard boxes to make a fort with, old
clothes for dress up, and other items that could be recycled
into play things.*

*Much of my playtime was outside whenever the
weather permitted. When weather didn't permit we
sometimes went outside anyway! Having to stay inside
was almost a punishment! AND I WAS HAPPY!!!! If a
friend had a new toy or game I didn't feel deprived, left
out or jealous since we all played together and usually
shared everything.*

Great irony exists when we consider that a child growing up
during the Great Depression would be much less likely to suffer
from depression than one growing up with all our modern affluence.
America may be the greatest producer and consumer of resources,
but we also have the highest divorce rate, obesity rate, and depression
rate in the world. Something is clearly broken.[1]

Finding Enough in our Culture of Excess

According to the book by Thomas J. Stanley and William D. Danko,
The Millionaire Next Door, the profession that has the highest
percentage of millionaires is not doctors, lawyers, or professional
sports players. It is actually auctioneers. That's right. The guy who
is selling stuff for, "Ten dollars, ten dollars. Who'll give me ten
dollars?" is actually more likely to be a millionaire than the doctor
next door.[2] The doctor may earn large sums of money, but his net
worth is rarely as high as the auctioneer's.

This is because auctioneers understand the concept of Enough. Their job is to go from business to business and estate to estate selling things for one tenth or less of their original value, because someone else didn't understand Enough. Auctioneers usually own their own companies and choose to live differently than other businessmen because they witness daily the brevity and the worthlessness of stuff.

On the other hand, athletes with million dollar salaries and even extreme lottery winners often struggle with covering their expenses. According to a 2010 study by researchers at Vanderbilt and Kentucky Universities, the more money people win in the lottery, the more likely they are to end up bankrupt. The National Endowment for Financial Education found similar results and estimated that 70 percent of people who unexpectedly come into large sums of money ended up broke within seven years. [3]

As parents, we must understand these statistics and studies so that we can teach against the culture trying to woo our children by get rich quick stories. Certainly no one would celebrate a "*These people are going to face intense pain and hardship over the next seven years—they just don't know it yet*," story. A 2008 Carnegie Mellon University study found something called the "peanuts effect."[4] When participants were given one dollar at a time and asked whether they'd like to spend it on a lottery ticket, many more chose to do so than those in the other group who were given $5 and asked if they'd like to spend it *all* on lottery tickets. In other words, some sums of money are so small that we tend to assume they don't even count. But they do count.

The reality is that if the low-income families who "invest" $200 a year in lottery tickets instead truly invested that money, even at a 3% interest rate, they would have $10,000 in 30 years. Though we are not trying to raise misers or hoarders, we must help our children understand that how we spend money matters, and we must make financial decisions based on wisdom rather than what we think others are doing with their money.

One couple who had been earning close to $250,000 for a few years in a row complained of feeling stressed by their debts and frustrated about how this large sum of money still left them feeling "poor." After we asked them a few questions, they realized they had never planned where their money would go. It simply seemed like it should have been enough to satisfy their expenses, but it wasn't. Quickly they devised a balanced spending plan and began to make progress.

Just a few weeks after we met with them, however, one of their neighbors awkwardly approached them for financial advice. "You guys really look like you have your finances buttoned up, and we could use some financial advice. We just can't seem to make it from paycheck to paycheck." So in their vast neighborhood of large homes and luxury cars, at least two families were struggling, but each mistakenly thought they were the only ones.

If we raise children who have an understanding of Enough, we can be confident that they will be able to manage their own finances one day, no matter what salary they earn. By managing their experiences in the early, formative years, we can minimize the deceptive draw of our culture that yearns for more, more, more.

CHAPTER 7

MANAGING THEIR ENVIRONMENT

"That's so sad. That kid just wasted about five bucks on that grab-claw machine. I don't get why he would put any money in that machine any way. What if he actually won one of those big, cheap bears?" Any one of my four boys could have shared these comments with me. Time and life have blurred the exact details of this memory, but the quote is crystal clear. My child saw the grab-claw machine in a way that its creators never intended. Despite the allure of lights and the multi-colored stuffed animals and its convenient placement in the waiting area in Denny's, this machine did not seduce my child into playing it. Instead, he was saddened by the other child's loss of resources.

One of our most powerful tools in combating materialism in our children is the ability to manage our children's environment. In their very early years of life, we have almost complete control over where our children go, what they see, and what they do. It will be over a decade before they will actually have enough resources and mobility to buy anything we don't approve of or participate in any activity we don't feel is beneficial to them. How we introduce them to new experiences during these early years is critical.

Unpacking the Grab-Claw Machine

As every new experience presents itself, we have the ability to share with our children a perspective by which to view the experience. Let's take a look at what this perspective could be for the grab-claw machine. For years, it's easy enough to ignore the grab-claw machine and others like it. It easily fades into the background of life. If we don't draw attention to it or give it power, a child will likely be four or five years old before they begin to get curious about it. Once they notice it, we can then guide them to an understanding that:

1) The machine is specifically designed to rarely grab a prize.
2) The prizes are worth very little—often less than the cost of playing.
3) We don't have any use or need for the item in the machine.
4) The machine is quite similar to gambling in that the player often ends up spending more just trying to "win" something for "free."
5) If they actually wanted what was in the machine, it would be wiser to save the money and go buy it.

The opposite is also true. If we hold up an 18-month-old to the machine and point out all the cool goodies inside, we begin nurturing an interest and then very quickly a desire to play the game. If we give quarters to the three-year-old each time we come across the machine, we quickly train them to ask for money every time they see it. We also train them to have a subconscious desire for the stuff inside the machine and a new awareness of the possibility of getting something for nothing.

Certainly, this machine possesses no inherently evil qualities. Children who play the machine are not *all* fooled by its allure. Some actually just want to have a little fun for a quarter or two. The problem comes when the children spend quarter after quarter and dollar after dollar, giving the machine the power to take the money right out of their pockets—or their moms' purses. The problem comes when the stuff inside becomes something they are willing to exchange a lot of money to obtain.

Have you ever looked at the merchandise inside those machines? You usually won't find plush, sweet-looking, stuffed animals. No. They are hard, Styrofoam bead-packed, creepy-eyed creatures. Some you can't even decide if they are animal or monster with their over-sized features and bright colors. Other favorite objects inside these machines are random jewelry. Really, do you want your child "winning" a piece of jewelry that a metal claw picked-out? I imagine it would be only hours before the chain broke or the stuffed animal started leaking tiny white beads in my house.

A second problem comes when children become conditioned to play these machines whenever they see them. This habit, once created, can be broken by a strong parental response like, "You know what? That stuff is junky, and we have enough stuff already. I'm not going to let you waste my money on that anymore. If you want to spend your money, you need to tell me ahead of time exactly how much you plan to spend, and tell me before you see the machine. We came to Denny's for breakfast, not to be tricked out of our money."

The same logic is true for grown women at the Cracker Barrel Restaurant (a national chain that features an elaborate gift shop in the waiting area). You show up for a pancake and walk out with a scented candle. Decide what you will buy before you see it. If you do decide to buy the scented candle, let your kids know, "I have been looking for a present for Aunt Amy's birthday. She will love this."

The Power of Modeling

In no way do I want to suck the joy out of shopping at the Cracker Barrel gift shop. I also don't want to create any paranoia that buying a random present for yourself or someone else will send your kids on a path to financial ruin. Instead, I'm hoping you'll recognize the power you innately possess simply by modeling wise stewardship. When your kids see you being content, they will learn contentment. Likewise, if they regularly see you examining every single buying opportunity in search of something to purchase, then they, too, will examine every buying opportunity.

Our kids could easily develop a habit of "hobby shopping," if we repeatedly model it for them. Teen and tween girls, in particular, can make shopping their favorite recreational activity, that thing they do for fun, the exclusive way they connect with their friends. Rather than focusing on their friend's depth of character and favorite hobbies, these girls spend all their time conquering the malls weekly and end up limiting their social relationships to how cute their friend's outfit is.

Offer these girls the insight that fashions are constantly changing—it's the game companies play to keep us buying new things. And if we spend all our time worrying about making our outsides look stylish, we can easily neglect our insides. Boys and girls both must hear our messages about inner beauty and character.

Our power in modeling also includes our ability to model contentment or discontentment to our kids. As youngsters, our kids seem to innately ask us, "Hey, how come we don't have a _____?" You can fill in the blank with just about anything—a pool, a bigger house, a trampoline, or a dog. Our response will either model contentment or discontentment. We can say, "I wish we could . . . " or "That would sure be nice . . . " These responses send the message that those things would make our lives better, fuller, happier. How much stronger it would be if we modeled contentment

> *Our responses will either model contentment or discontentment*

for our kids: "Those things would probably be fun for a little while, but then we would get used to them and want something else, the next new thing we saw. I want to always appreciate what we have and not be chasing what we don't have."

The Power of Conditioning

Russian Physiologist Ivan Pavlov was able to demonstrate the power of classical conditioning in his famous experiment with his dog. Over a period of time, he would ring a bell immediately before feeding his dog. After only a few repetitions, the dog anticipated the food and began to salivate at the sound of the bell alone.[1] Likewise, we must recognize how *we* condition the habits and desires of our children.

I will never forget starting to realize this a few days after returning from a trip to Florida, when the boys were still little. To make time pass more quickly on the 18-hour drive, we let them go into the gas station and pick out a treat each time we stopped for gas in a new state. They greatly anticipated each stop and enjoyed their suckers or pretzels for extended periods of time after. My husband and I reveled at the genius of our plan.

A few days after we arrived back home, I stopped to get gas. All the boys bounded out of the car and dashed into the gas station. "What are you guys doing?" I asked.

"We're going in to pick out our treat," Michael explained with resolution. A reality check quickly followed, and they sulked back to the car empty-handed. How quickly they'd become conditioned to assume that a gas station stop meant a treat!

In what ways have you conditioned a response to a given situation? Do your children expect you to buy them any of the following?:

- a treat at the store
- a replacement toy when one breaks
- some books from the school book order
- a toy from a gift shop or toy store

- popcorn at the movies
- a gumball at the gumball machine
- all new clothes every September
- the latest, greatest trendy *"thing"*

Do your children expect any of these?:

- a vacation every spring break
- an extravagant birthday party with fifteen of their closest friends
- $20 to spend at the arcade
- a trip to McDonald's when they're hungry
- a trip to the latest movie at the theater each weekend

Until we recognize and claim the incredible power we have to influence a child's environment, we will struggle in our efforts to minimizing their pursuit of stuff.

Navigating Mine Fields of Discontent

The Checkout Line: These narrow store aisles should be marked with yellow, caution tape warning parents: *Your young child is about to ask you for something. Proceed with caution.* Until the child has enough language skills to actually ask for something, you should simply ignore all the treats on display. As soon as the child begins to ask with a word or a reach, answer with authority, "No, we didn't come here to buy that today."

As they mature, teach them why stores put those items there. Talk about impulse buys—items the stores strategically place near the checkout where you'll have to wait in line for who knows how long. Obviously, they hope you buy these items without thinking. On your next trip to the store, take a look at the items they choose to display there. Why did the store choose these particular items? Why not green beans? Note: If these items are on your list, purchasing them wouldn't qualify as an impulse buy.

When my son Bryan was about eight, he had some allowance money he wanted to spend on a Twix candy bar at Target. Having been well versed in the store's marketing techniques from a young age, Bryan felt obliged to share something with the distracted checkout lady, much to my embarrassment. "Excuse me, but I wanted you to know that I planned on buying this candy bar, even before I came in that door." The checkout lady was not quite sure what he was talking about, but I knew my son didn't want her to think he was tricked into buying it. He made a logical decision, not an impulse buy.

Arcades: Whether quietly tucked away in the back of a bowling alley or proudly displayed with flashing lights and whirling sounds on Main Street, arcades attract kids of all ages. The lights and sounds draw them in like moths to flutter from Skee-Ball to Dance Dance Revolution to Whack-a-Mole. Arcades are not that different from casinos. Children cash in their mom's $20 in hopes of winning the giant blow-up guitar or the over-sized, dusty pink rabbit for 25,000 tickets.

But, as parents, we have the power to manage this. We can teach our kids that arcades certainly can be fun, but are not a *good deal*. Exchanging a couple of dollars for a spin on a big wheel where they might win enough tickets to buy 3 Tootsie Rolls is suddenly silly. Two dollars can buy three candy bars at Wal-Mart. Exchanging $20 for 20 Tootsie Rolls would qualify as downright wasteful. Similarly, $20 can buy four movie tickets at a matinee. However, if your family chooses this as your entertainment for the night and the kids have set out to spend $20 for the evening's fun, then let them try it. If—or, more accurately, *when*—the fun last only a few minutes, they'll catch on quickly enough.

We avoided arcades for years by explaining that we didn't think it was a good deal. Sure, the boys had glimpsed them briefly at kids' birthday parties and had occasionally used a dollar or two of their own money at a mini-arcade, but we never gave them our money (no matter how much they begged).

One night, on a vacation, we decided to make our point. We told the boys they could each have $5 to play whatever games they wanted at the boardwalk arcade. Within minutes, all four kids were broke. They combined the tickets they "won" and exchanged them for a handful of Dum Dum suckers. As we walked back to our cottage, Andy and I stopped to buy two ice cream cones.

"Why only two?" one of them asked. "Do we have to have a sharing buddy?" That term is one of our family's little secrets that the older boys still tease us about from their childhood of having to share the same cone with a brother.

"No guys. These treats are for Mom and Dad. You spent your ice cream money at the arcade." Mean? A little. But they got the point. They learned that spending money comes down to making choices. On the last night of vacation we asked who wanted to go to the arcade and who wanted to get the giant ice cream cones. All four kids chose ice cream, and the lure of an arcade lost its grip on them that night.

Birthday Parties: Back in the day, birthday parties meant having a few close friends over to the house for cake and ice cream and maybe a little Pin-the-Tail-on-the-Donkey for some added excitement. Now it is the norm to invite the entire class, plan an excursion, and provide goodie bags to the kids (who just received an afternoon of fun paid for by you). Typical kids' parties can cost parents hundreds of dollars for the two-hour event, which may or may not include whining and tears by at least one child who is not happy with the way things are going at your all-expense paid birthday extravaganza.

We chose not to enter into that madness for a couple of reasons. First, my boys only had a couple of close friends throughout elementary school. Inviting more than three or four kids didn't make sense. I also never wanted to entertain (read: corral) a houseful of children, each armed with a $15-$25 gift. We had enough toys and didn't need 10 more at one sitting. The culture changed anyway, and by the time my youngest had his last birthday party, kids were bringing gift cards rather than gifts, which seemed to have stripped away the personal aspect of gift-giving.

Celebrating with a big party is great for those parents who enjoy this kind of event. One of my best friends is a caterer and she loved throwing large, themed parties when our kids were little. These events certainly felt like they were catered, with every detail reflecting each year's clever theme. The kids and I had a blast attending. To my friend, those kinds of parties were fun and effortless, but I would never have been able to pull off a party like hers. And that's OK. If you don't have the enthusiasm, expertise, or budget to make it happen, then don't do it—and release yourself from the guilt. What is right for one family may not necessarily be right for yours.

My neighbor lets her kids have a "friend party" every other year. Another friend has special parties at ages 5, 10, and 16. One year, Matthew wanted to have a big party at a laser tag place. Rather than booking the party package for $200-plus, we simply brought the kids in to play (with a coupon) and then returned home for cake and ice cream, paying less than half the price of the party package. Birthdays are exciting for kids no matter what. We don't need to bust our budgets to make them fun.

Christmas: This holiday has been strategically and tragically altered over the years, morphing from a celebration of the birth of our Savior into a season of overspending and obsessing over insignificant details. Instead of taking time to reflect on Christ's birth, we become crazy busy, running around in search of the perfect teacher gifts and scheduling just the right breakfast with Santa. Creating an atmosphere of peace and simplicity during this hectic time is a gift and a blessing to our families. Christmas doesn't have to mean crazy. Take a stand.

Because the Christmas season can still be hectic despite our best efforts, one of my friends bakes her Christmas cookies on New Year's Day. With the Christmas rush behind her, she is able to thoroughly enjoy her two young children on a day when the only activity is baking cookies and watching football. Baking Christmas cookies on New Year's Day became not an oddity, but a much-anticipated tradition for her kids. Other people reduce the frenzy by shopping in October or sending out New Year's cards rather than Christmas cards.

I know some couples who give their kids just three gifts, just like the Bible mentions Jesus got. Others focus on giving to families in need during this time. For us, I like to have Christmas be the time to buy things the boys will need during the upcoming year rather than dumping piles of new toys on them. New coats, sweaters, shoes, and t-shirts make great gifts. When they were little, Christmas stockings were filled with Elmo bubble bath, Thomas the Tank undies, and new crayons and coloring books. As teenagers, their stockings now contain acne pads, deodorant, Chapstick, and gum. And Christmas morning is still exciting. Again, establish and manage your family's expectations of the holiday season.

A discussion about Christmas wouldn't be complete without at least one mention of the "Hot Christmas Toy" phenomenon. For decades, parents all over the U.S. have been doing crazy things to locate and/or overpay for the hot toy of the season. Often times the toy is marketed for kids too young to even ask for it. And what if they do ask for it? That just provides you with an awesome opportunity to teach: "That toy is overpriced, hard to find, and something nobody will enjoy within a month of receiving it. Our family doesn't do crazy."

Like birthdays, Christmas is special and exciting in itself. Decide where you want to set the financial bar at Christmas. It really doesn't have to mean spending hundreds, or even thousands of dollars on your children. Consider your own Christmas memories from childhood. I know that mine include the things we did—baking cookies, singing Christmas carols at church, and decorating the tree—rather than the specific gifts I received. Christmas is the season of giving. Give your children the gift of a simple Christmas filled with peace and love.

Toy Catalogs: I'll never forget the Christmas I made a huge mistake. Because of their limited exposure to TV, magazine ads, and the Target toy aisle, my four sons rarely had a definitive response to the question posed to all little kids during this season: "So, what do you want for Christmas?" They always responded: candy, gum, and more candy. But Grandma and the aunts wanted a better answer than that. They wanted to buy their grandkids and nephews something more exciting. So when the Toys "R" Us catalog arrived in the mail the following week, I ceremoniously presented them with four different color highlighters and the mission to find some things they each liked. Big mistake. Huge. By the time I reclaimed the catalog, it bled a rainbow of neon yellow, orange, green, and blue.

This experience solidified in my mind the truth that my little guys were only one catalog away from being incredibly discontent. After seeing how quickly their wish lists overflowed with new wants, I promised to wait until they had a firmer understanding of the fleeting joy stuff provides before I tempted them with another toy catalog. Grandma and the aunts know my boys. They can always figure out what to buy that they'll enjoy. So when Grandma bought all four of them giant Nerf dart guns one year, I smiled as they ambushed each other for weeks. Grandma didn't need a wish list. She just needed to know them. And she did.

Over the years, my sons have matured and grown in their understanding of the limited joy that stuff provides. They can look at a catalog now and make decisions based on a clear understanding of their wants and needs. I remember the year I asked Bryan if he had some ideas about what he might like for Christmas. "I don't know what I want—but I know what I *don't* want: no more stuffed animals, no more Legos, no more games . . . " He was on the verge of being a teenager that year, and he was making a clean break from his childhood desires.

I understand the power of Pavlov. We, too, have the power to condition our kids away from the culture of stuff and towards the joy of family and friends. If we manage their environment strategically, we will have the freedom to walk peacefully by gumball machines without fear of tantrums. We will be able to shop for other kids' birthday presents without incident at the toy store. We will be able to eat Cheerios out of the box in the car when we're hungry rather than stopping for fast food. And we will be certain that no one in our family is overly concerned with the latest, greatest thing. So, be wise. Recognize your influence, and shape how your kids see their world.

Chapter 8

CREATING A FINANCIAL FILTER

While substitute teaching at my boys' middle school a few years ago, I passed by a crowded lunch table of giggly girls. Around a table sat eight cheerleaders, eight ponytails, sixteen UGG boots, and one package of Pop-Tarts. I asked the girl with my favorite Brown Cinnamon Pop-Tart, "Hey, I didn't know they sold those here. How much are they?"

With a flip of the ponytail and a smirk of the upper lip she responded, "Uh, how should I know?" After remembering that I was an adult with enough self-respect to pick myself up from this verbal slap, I realized that something was very wrong here. This girl had no financial filter to pass decisions through. She saw a Pop-Tart. She wanted the Pop-Tart. She bought the Pop-Tart using her magical student ID card with mystical financial powers built right in. The price of the Pop-Tart didn't concern her.

Cafeteria workers across our school district confirm that the majority of students aren't concerned at all with the price of the items they purchase. With daily regularity, many students purchase bottled water for $1.25 extra or Gatorade for $1.50 extra. Often they never finish these drinks because they have only about 20 minutes to eat lunch. Workers sometimes have to remind students that their lunch does not contain certain needed food groups, which means students have to pay higher a la carte prices. Their only response?

"Do I have enough money on my card?" If they have enough money on their card, they buy the items, despite being charged twice what a regular lunch would cost.

Why does this matter? What's so wrong with a 13-year-old feeling hungry and buying some food without knowing the price? At some point, sooner rather than later, kids must learn they cannot have everything they want. And since money is not limitless, decisions must be made about where and how to spend it wisely. They need to learn that some things are a good deal and some things are not. They need a reference point for how much things cost so they can compare prices on similar items and recognize, "This is not a good value, but I'm really hungry so I'm going to get it anyway."

Small Choices Really Do Matter

I remember the look of confusion on my husband's face when I asked him why he bought grapes at $2.99 a pound. Since he was not the usual shopper and was just trying to be helpful by picking up some fruit on his way home, he had no idea that a good price for grapes is $1.29 a pound. Or that $.99 a pound means you fill your cart with grapes while $2.99 a pound means no grapes this week. But that day, because I was able to provide a pricing context, my husband adjusted his financial filter to include the price of grapes.

Absolutely, we could have afforded $8.32 worth of grapes. But what if he had done the same thing at the meat counter, in the cookie aisle, and in the Diet Coke aisle? What if he had not considered any of the prices on things he bought? If we go through the day with no concept that any of these decisions are important, then we can easily be deceived into thinking these small choices don't matter. But they do.

Getting a car wash weekly or purchasing Starbucks daily adds up. Decisions like these snowball, so that by the end of the year many families are surprised that their credit card balances have not been paid off like they had hoped. Rather, they've sunk even further into the quicksand of consumer debt. Yet the reverse is also true if families instead make many small, wise decisions. It matters. Consider a family that cuts $100 a week of unnecessary expenses (eliminate one fast food trip, no full-priced grocery meat, no trip to the movies for the whole family). That's $5,200 by the end of the year that can be used to pay off debt. Also don't forget these are post-tax dollars, which means the person would need to earn somewhere between $5,778-$8,667 to spend the $5,200 in the first place.

Having a financial filter to pass decisions through is what will keep families on the road to financial freedom rather than financial ruin.

Questions for Wise Consumers

In order to develop into wise consumers, kids must be taught to create their own filter to pass all financial decisions through. The following questions are helpful for both child and parent alike:

- Do I need this?
- Do I *really* want this, or will I grow tired of it soon?
- Is it worth the money, or could I find it cheaper somewhere else?
- What else could/should I buy with this money?

Do I Need This?

Kids must first understand the difference between a *want* and a *need*. Sure, my son needs new shoes, but he wants shoes with wheels. Understanding this difference is foundational.

In 1983, companies spent $100 million marketing to kids. Today, they're spending nearly $17 billion annually. That's more than double what it was in 1992.[1] All this to try to convince kids that their every want is actually a need. If we listen to the marketers, babies *need* specialized black and white toys to stimulate their little brains lest they fall behind. Kids *need* a Wii because all the other neighborhood kids have an absolute blast on theirs and it gives kids exercise. Teenage girls *need* shorts the length of a pencil from Abercrombie and Fitch so they can be popular and the boys will like them. Teenage boys *need* $200 tennis shoes because That Kid just bought some and he's the best athlete in the school. (Sarcasm intended.)

Helping kids use the correct word when asking for something begins the very first time they say, "Mom, I need a Happy Meal." What they meant to say was, "I want a Happy Meal," or "I need something to eat," because no one *needs* a Happy Meal. A friend of mine who had been doing some training in this area with her six-year-old son let me know about one of her setbacks. After leaving Target he announced, "The real problem is that I need everything that I want."

Do I really want this, or will I grow tired of it soon?

Once they understand they *want* something rather than needing it, have them determine how much they want it. How long have they been thinking about it? Why do they want it? Do other kids have it, and might that be why they want it so much? How much will they use it? If it's food or an experience, what would happen if they just didn't get it?

One great option for helping kids think through a decision is creating "The List." This is a place where we list things that we want to think more about before buying them. When your child first begins asking for things to buy, tell him to, "Put it on your list." Explain that even Mom and Dad have a list of things we are thinking about buying. As he gets get older, share with him some things that are on your list.

When Christopher was about six, he cradled a GI Joe guy in his arms at the store. He gazed up at me with his precious blue eyes and spider eyelashes and stated longingly, "This guy has been on my list... since the day I was born." Since it clearly was not on his list, GI Joe stayed at the store—and was quickly forgotten.

We tried to keep the list figurative rather than literal for that reason. My thinking was that if you couldn't remember what was on your list, then it shouldn't be on there any longer. Having a child "put it on their list" is a first step in delayed gratification training (Chapter 11), yet it also makes them feel that their interest is heard and that you take their preferences seriously.

I have also made a point of keeping those trinkets that passed through the filter of the list but ended up being a disappointment, a learning experience rather than a great purchase. These have included: a set of mini highlighters, an eraser the size of my foot, a plastic dog on skates, and rubber wading boots. When a child is considering a purchase, and I see that it might not be all they dream it will be, I share my stash of their past, erroneous decisions to help them determine if there might be a similarity.

Is it worth the money? Could I find it cheaper somewhere else?

Your kids should consider these critical question before they actually make a purchase. They are on the verge of exchanging some of their limited resources for something else, and they need to think through whether this purchase is a good value. Value training can begin as soon as the child can understand your words. Grocery stores were my favorite training ground in those early years. At least twice a week for months and then years, my kids would hear, "Well, how much is it? No, not today," "Yes, that's a good price. Get a couple of them," or "Have we tried the generic brand on this yet? It's 59 cents cheaper." The boys could hear my financial filter at work prior to making decisions.

Very quickly we learned that there is no generic equal for Honey Nut Cheerios and off-brand Pop-Tarts are just plain wrong. Generic pasta saves us 29 cents a box and generic gallons of milk can save us $1.00. By the time each of my boys reached the age of ten, I was able to send them to another part of the grocery store to choose items we needed from the options on the shelf. They had learned that little decisions matter.

Developing this financial filter also includes helping them understand the laws of supply and demand. While I would never spend $1.50 for a Diet Coke at a gas station near our home (when the Coke in my pantry is 21 cents each), I have on occasion spent that much when I was hot, with a caffeine headache, and hours away from a value-priced Diet Coke. However, I am unable to pay $4.50 for a Coke at a movie theater or sporting event. Ever. My body loses all love of the drink at that price. The only things I can see in my mind are four 2-liter bottles of Diet Coke lined up next to the 16oz. cup for $4.50. Yet, I do spend close to $125 to have my hair cut and highlighted, and I gladly pay $45 an hour for my son's piano lessons. But when I listen to his lesson, I drink a 21 cent Coke from home.

What else could I buy with the money?

Remember this key principle: The amount of money will always be limited, and the options of things to buy will always be limitless. This "rule" holds true for adults as well. Consider what else you could buy. Sure, a timeshare or vacation home might be tempting, but after adding all the costs, would earlier retirement be more valuable? A snowmobile or boat sounds exciting, but after piling on all the added costs beyond the initial price, would less financial stress be more thrilling? We considered a boat once. The boys love

> *The amount of money will always be limited, and the options of things to buy will always be limitless.*

to fish, and we had a barn to store it. But after listing all the costs and discussing how much we would actually use it, we decided to rent a boat whenever we really wanted to go. That way, we could test how much we would enjoy it before making such a big commitment. We've rented a boat exactly once.

The Dangers of No Financial Filter

Kids without solid financial filters make poor financial choices. They also tend to not take care of the things they already have. Bikes rust in the rain; toys break with aggressive play; game pieces are lost. If a toy does break, they expect a replacement. If they lose their book for school, they expect parents to cough up the cash without a hint of remorse or wrongdoing. Kids without a financial filter of any sort are at a high risk for future misfortune with personal finances.

In our counseling sessions, we commonly see families who have absolutely no financial filter. When they have a large tax refund due to arrive soon, they begin dreaming about the vacation they can now take or the home improvement project they can complete. Unfortunately, most carry a significant consumer debt load at interest rates upwards of 20 percent, so they would actually pay for their dreams with debt, even though it feels like they are paying with cash from the refund.

Few couples in credit card debt really understand this concept. One family carried over $23,000 on a variety of credit cards, having played the credit card shuffle for six years with no reduction of the principle. One spring, this couple had a $5,230 tax refund securely in hand, and they shared their plans for a family vacation in six months. After much discussion, we convinced them to apply the entire amount of the tax refund to their credit card debt balance. Then we encouraged them to set up a special account to save from their current spending for the vacation. We didn't want to be dream killers, so we told them when it came time for their vacation, if they needed more money they could simply pay with their credit card. "What? Pay for the trip with our credit card?" they gasped. "We'd never charge a vacation on a credit card."

But this is *exactly* what any family is doing when they "pay cash" for a vacation or spa visit or home improvement while they are still carrying credit card debt. This family saved $535 in interest payments alone on the $5,230 they removed from their credit card balance. With that little taste of freedom, this family did save a smaller amount in the six-month time frame and chose a more modest vacation so they would not have to put more money on their credit cards. They tasted freedom, and they liked it.

While on an airplane, flight attendants instruct passengers to "Put on your own oxygen mask first before helping small children." Similarly, parents must have their own financial filter securely in place before they can help their children create theirs. For kids to be grateful and capable of managing their own finances some day, they must see parents who resist temptations from the world, who make decisions about where their money goes, and who plan for the future.

Spending Plans: The Ultimate Financial Filter

In our ten years of counseling couples who were drowning in debt and experiencing stressed lives and stressed marriages, we never met with a couple who was currently working from a budget. Many of them *said* they had a budget but it "just wasn't working." Upon closer inspection, the budget they referred to was simply a list of their expenses for each month.

Lists of expenses are passive. Budgets are active. They define exactly what the family intends to spend each month. A list of purchases is simply a recording of what happened, more than likely without much of any other financial filter in place. One couple we met with had spent $350 on eating out one month and had bounced a number of checks resulting in over $100 in bank fees. They felt stressed about whether they could make the boat payment the following month, if they didn't get their home equity line in time.

Developing a household-spending plan (*budget* often sounds restricting to people, and they quit before even getting started) is wise for parents, but children also benefit from seeing a family empowered to spend their resources with wisdom and forethought. Teach your children that all multi-million and -billion dollar companies have spending plans. Explain that it is a way to keep the company on solid financial ground while also having an eye open for future growth.

While children do not need to know every detail of the family's budget, they will benefit from understanding the priorities that have been set. They should also see and hear Mom and Dad discussing the household finances so they can see that it takes teamwork and planning. When our sons were much younger and asked for something we had not planned on getting them, we explained to them that we were focusing on paying the house off. They accepted this as a suitable goal because of prior conversations about debt and freedom. They would even correct each other at times, and say something like, "C'mon, Matty, what are you thinking? You can't get that—we're trying to pay off the house!"

However, only a few decades ago, discussing money matters with kids was taboo. For generations, parents kept the family's finances between husband and wife. Fortunately for them, this practice did little harm because when the kids grew up with families of their own, it was still fairly easy to manage finances. People had jobs that paid money, and then they spent money on things they needed. Pretty simple. No realtor was telling clients that for no money down they could live in a $500,000 house. No credit card company was sending $1,000 in case they needed a little extra cash one month. Television shows weren't constantly importing images of how other people lived in their "cribs" with their walk-in-closets lined with designer clothes.

My dad once told me he had no idea he was classified as low-income growing up in the inner-city of Cleveland because everyone else on his block had the same amount of money and had the same types of possessions. Now our kids feel poor if they don't have an air hockey table in their finished basement.

A well-orchestrated spending plan will not only help a family avoid the threat of debt, but it will also enable them to achieve financial goals that they thought were impossible with the passive "list my expenses" program.

Budget Basics

To be effective, the plan must 1) balance and 2) allocate money toward *expected* unexpected categories. The car will need repairs; you're just not sure when. Someone will run into the corner of the wall and need stitches costing $628; you're just not exactly sure who, when, or which wall. The garbage disposal will need to be replaced at some point, and one of the kids will need glasses or braces or need a dermatologist. By allocating this money each month and keeping it in a special account, families are less likely to resort to credit card debt to get by when those events actually occur.

Kids and adults alike must also realize that many decisions that don't appear to involve money *are* financial decisions, which need a financial filter. If a child wants to play soccer or join the school band, finances will be involved. If they want to make a special trip across town to get a forgotten book, gas will cost money. And remember that boat we wanted to buy? Its cost was not limited to the sticker price. Boat insurance, storage fees, winterizing fees, docking fees, maintenance fees, a trailer, gas, and entertaining expenses all add to the real cost of a boat.

Help your child make the connection between all these choices and their financial implications. Doing so will help them understand that the real cost of their wants is often much higher than they realize. Most children want a puppy. But the total cost of the new puppy is certainly not just the initial cost to take him home. Instead a family will spend thousands of dollars on a dog over his lifetime, for things like food, vet bills, boarding bills, chew toys, a crate, and the stuff he destroys when not in his crate.

When we were first married, I told my dad how excited Andy and I were to buy a dog. He answered my enthusiasm with some pragmatism, "A dog? You just got married! A dog is nothing more than a hole to throw money in." We still bought the dog. We loved the dog. But the dog cost far more over his ten-year lifetime than we ever anticipated. So before I get attacked by dog lovers of the world, of which we are members, my point is that we must raise children who understand the financial implications of decisions that might not look like financial decisions at first glance.

With this ultimate financial filter in place, you can raise children who participate in the success of the spending plan. After a growth spurt, give each child a fixed amount to buy new clothes for school. In September, give each child money for school supplies. If this money is limited and reasonable, each child will be forced to make decisions through their new filters. This will make the latest-teen-heart-throb folders not quite as appealing as the blue, red, and yellow ones that cost one tenth as much.

At our kids' schools they give parents the option of buying all their child's school supplies from a company for one price. A busy person—with limited time for chasing around a pink pearl eraser and 3x3 Post-It notes—might consider this a great option, something that would definitely pass through their financial filter. Yet if you know most of the clerks in Wal-Mart by name, shopping the loss leaders with your kids can be a great learning opportunity. Loss leaders are those items that stores actually sell below the wholesale price just to get customers in their doors. Back-to-school shopping is the perfect time to teach your kids about this concept.

One year I gave my boys the exact amount that the school was charging for their school supply kits. I told them they had to buy everything on the list, and they could keep the difference they saved to spend on whatever they wanted. Unfortunately, that strategy worked for that year only; the next year my sons insisted they really didn't need *anything* new and asked me to just give them the cash. I get it. Skittles and Slushies are quite a bit more exciting than new glue sticks and crayons.

The Financial Filter—to the Extreme

Emphasizing the importance of always being discerning shoppers does have its drawbacks. One year when Michael and Bryan were around eight and nine, I had them get dressed for swimming lessons in a locker room for families. The room was packed with dads and moms trying to get wiggly children squeezed into bathing suits or back into street clothes. From across the room I heard an outraged voice remark, "Twenty-five cents for a napkin? Bry, come here and look. Who would pay twenty-five cents for a napkin?"

As my mind registered what was going on and I started the slow-motion dash across the locker room, the voice continued, "Mom! How many napkins do you think you get for a quarter? It doesn't make sense since you can get them free if you just ask for extra at the drive-thru . . . " By the time I reached them, all eyes were upon me as I explained to my sons that those were special napkins and actually a very good deal for a quarter.

~~∞∞∞~~

I remember being at an open house for a home over 15 years ago. The realtor spoke with a well-dressed man who didn't seem satisfied with the house we were all touring. He asked the potential buyer, "Well, what price range are you looking at?" His reply was one I will never forget.

"No limit," he announced.

Are we raising our kids with limits? And not just restrictive, "we're-so-sad-we're-on-a-budget" limits. But empowering, self-imposed limits that will in actuality provide them with the freedom to choose where and how they live.

Next Steps:

1. Create a family spending plan if you do not have one already. Crown.org has useful tips and has access to local financial counselors. It's almost impossible for kids to have a financial filter if their parents do not have one.

2. List all debts from smallest to largest, including the mortgage. Though potentially scary at first, bringing the information out into the light is freeing. Just because you don't look at it doesn't mean it goes away. Dave Ramsey's *Total Money Makeover* outlines how to effectively attack these debts one at a time with the Debt Snowball.

3. This week, be sure to model for your kids the questions you ask before buying something.

4. Discuss the following questions with your spouse:

    - How can our family's spending plan empower our family and provide a framework for determining how much is Enough?

    - How can we communicate our plan to our children in an age-appropriate way?

    - What first step can we take today to continue our walk away from financial stress and toward financial freedom?

    - Specifically, how will we model this for our children to effectively show them our own financial filter so they can witness first-hand how one works?

Chapter 9

MINIMIZING THE INFLOW OF STUFF

My sister called recently and asked me if I knew anyone who would like a giant bag full of toys for their young kids. She had decluttered her basement and was ready to bestow a blessing on a young family. The only problem was I couldn't think of anyone. Not one family I knew needed more toys. No one she knew needed more toys. She even tried to donate them to a local thrift store, but a sign on the front door announced, "No longer accepting stuffed animals, board games, or toys with any missing pieces." Defeated, she dragged her bag back to the car and abandoned it at Goodwill, hoping that someone somewhere might find her cast-offs exciting.

Children living at almost any income level trip over stuffed bears and pea-sized Lego shrapnel on their way to their overflowing dressers each morning to get dressed for school. Bins of hair bows or stacks of baseball hats line many kids' closet shelves. The Container Store exists for the sole purpose of aiding people in their quest to organize their abundance of stuff.

According to Paul Graham, an essayist and business investor, "Your stuff is in fact worse than worthless, because once you've accumulated a certain amount of stuff, it starts to own you rather than the other way around. I know one couple who couldn't retire to the town they preferred because they couldn't afford a place there big enough for all their stuff. Their house isn't theirs; it's their stuff's." But why? Why do we accumulate so much stuff that it becomes work to keep it organized or even simply contained?

One reason is that the toys are cheap. Relatively speaking, with garage sales, second-hand stores, and the clearance bins, we can purchase items at very little cost to the budget. Family and friends help as well. I figured out the math once and realized that with four kids and two gift-giving occasions a year and twelve people who buy for them, our family receives 96 new things a year. This number also assumes that each person gives only one gift, which is not the case for a certain extra-generous grandmother.

A second reason it's so easy to accumulate stuff is because each purchase brings our kids joy—at least for a moment. And if our kids are happy, then we're happy—at least for a moment. We will continue to ensnare ourselves in the ongoing acquisition of stuff for our kids and stuff for ourselves until we admit that no purchase will ever bring us long-term joy.

Finally, we accumulate too much stuff because we don't even notice how it gets in. One day my son's nightstand had only a lamp and a book on it, and the next day it was littered with a pack of skeleton tattoos, a black and orange finger trap, a spider ring, and a sticky ghost that leaves marks when hurled at any painted surface. All this, compliments of a neighbor's Halloween party. Sure, I could have just waited a few days 'til the fun rubbed off; rather I used it as an opportunity to teach.

Developing an Eye for Junk

Keeping stuff from entering the house begins with training kids to have an eye for things that will break or things that won't be any fun after a short time. Rather than feign excitement for the plastic spider ring, talk about how you hope they will wear it and cherish it, but offer insight that it might just get lost or be unloved after a few days. Do the same for the other items from their goodie bag. Then wait and watch.

- Point out the typical lifecycle for items like these.
- Next, try to find all the party items after one week. Two weeks.
- How much joy did they bring after the first hour?
- Did anything break?
- Did the ghost leave marks on the walls or pick up fuzz from the carpet so that it became practically unusable?
- Is it a good use of natural resources to make these things and have them end up in the trash?

Wait, am I trying to create hoarders? Absolutely not. Some kids do cherish every balloon from the haircutting place and every paper placemat from Denny's. These kids (and I have one) need to recognize they can't cherish everything. The word *special* implies that something is different than the rest in some way. For kids who are natural hoarders, it is best to have bins, shelves, and containers that become "full." When the basket for stuffed animals is full in Christopher's room, he has to give away an animal before he adds a new one. Since one animal will have to go, the incoming stuffed animal must be more special than the one it is replacing. These kids will naturally treasure their possessions, so help them recognize that when the stuff becomes too much, we literally can't appreciate each item like we want.

Personally, I already have enough shoes in my closet. Decide for yourself how many that is. Since my designated shoe shelf is full, I find myself not buying a pair of new shoes because it's not fair to the pair of cute shoes that will have to leave my closet if the new ones come in. But when a pair of shoes has lived a full life, I can get pretty excited to shop for the replacement.

The treasure box at the dentist, the reward drawer at school, and the dollar bins at Target all tempt our kids to accumulate more stuff.

But to what end? Does the excitement last longer than a few days? Rarely. How often do these things break or not work like the child thought they would? The infamous Happy Meal is at least partially responsible for the play-and-toss culture we live in. Seriously—a toy for eating a burger and fries? Sure, sometimes these toys are cool enough that we may have actually paid money for them, but more often than not they filter to the bottom of the toy box to live in obscurity until a day of purging moves them to the trash. Have the courage to order a Happy Meal and say, "No toy, please." (Chick-fil-A will conveniently exchange a toy for an ice cream cone instead.) Train your kids to view these toys as junk. Train them to want to keep junk out of the house.

> *Train them to want to keep junk out of the house.*

The Great Purge

If we are going to make an effort to minimize the inflow of new stuff, we should also begin to cull the things we already have. Consider a child in another culture who has only a few, simple toys. Those toys would be treasured, cared for and truly appreciated. On the other hand, a child surrounded on all sides by tubs, bins, and shelves full of toys will be much less likely to feel the same.

Review with your kids the word "enough." Choose one area of the house, perhaps just a shelf, drawer, or dresser top. Take time to look at each toy or trinket. Where did it come from? Who bought it? Should it be kept or given to someone who would use it more? This process should be slow, steady, and take into account the emotional temperature of the child. Sure, I've snuck a few things out without approval and sent them in a care package to Brazil. But more often I have tried to gain the support of the item's current owner. Try Googling these words: organizing, decluttering, and minimalists. You'll find plenty of information in this area.

During this process, as you sort and organize and reminisce, remember to include each child's closet and dresser. These areas may not store toys, but they are places where excess can often hide. Like toys, clothes can also be cheap and challenging to decide how much is enough. I received so many adorable baby outfits as gifts for my first born that I quickly assumed a child actually needed a closet jammed with coordinating outfits and drawers brimming with t-shirts and matching shorts. But how many outfits can one child wear?

I remember packing up Michael's size nine-months clothes at the end of a season and finding quite a few things that he had only worn one time. I even found an outfit with tags still on it. How could he or I be grateful when we had so many things that he couldn't even wear them all once?

Over the years I have bought fewer and fewer clothes for my kids. Perhaps because they are boys, no one has even noticed. In reality, it seems that kids usually wear their favorite t-shirts and pants over and over again anyway. Once I asked Christopher when he was about 12-years-old how he decided what to wear each day. (I realized that I kept seeing the same couple t-shirts every week.) He stared at me with a puzzled look on his face and answered, "I wear whatever shirt is on top." This began my habit of rotating the laundry to the bottom of his drawer. I imagine girls probably don't choose outfits this same way.

Whether we have boys or girls, we need to decide how many clothes are enough. How many shoes are enough? When my sons were younger, we took a three-month camping trip throughout the western United States. Each of us took only one backpack with five t-shirts and three pairs of shorts. Incredibly, this felt like enough—though it was a year before I ever wanted to wear those clothes again once I returned home. Keeping articles of clothing at a reasonable quantity teaches children to be grateful for the clothes they have.

It can also limit their constant pursuit of the next outfit. One mom decided to tell her middle school daughter, "Just leave all the clothes you don't want on your closet or bedroom floor, and I will come by within 24 hours to take them to another girl your age who doesn't have this many clothes." This was after months of nagging her daughter to keep her extensive wardrobe off the floor. Sometimes, reducing the vast amount of clothes helps kids feel more grateful for the clothes they do have.

Clutter Training and Basic Organization 101

By age five or so, most children are able to understand concepts like clutter and organization. Taking care of our things is part of what we do when we are grateful for them. Stand at the doorway of each child's room with them and survey the landscape:

- Have them tell you what they see.
- Does everything have a place where it belongs?
- Are some dressers or end tables so full of stuff that they can't even be used?
- Is it easy to walk in the room without stepping on stuff?
- Does it seem like the person who lives here cares about their things?

Tell them you need to make sure that they don't have too much stuff. It's easy to tell what is too much because it is not loved enough to be cared for properly. It's too much if something doesn't have a specific place to belong. Ask them, "Would you feel cared for if you didn't have a place where you lived and belonged?" Depending on the amount of stuff, take a day, a week, or a month to be sure that everything in each child's room has a place. Whether or not a room is always clean and tidy is really for the parent and child to decide and work on together, separate from this exercise. But all children whose parents want them to be grateful must be able to organize their room when asked. The parent may choose to ask daily, weekly, or even monthly. But children age five and up *should* be able to put all their things where they belong without help.

Whiners and complainers may have too much stuff and may simply need to donate some of their things to kids who are more responsible. Younger kids should be purposefully (and cheerfully and patiently) trained in this area over time. The goal? To be able to independently clean their rooms by age five.

What about the child who insists he's "Not very good at putting things away"? Well, he must need more practice. I required my son who maintained he was organizationally-challenged to join me in organizing the basement, the garage, and the kitchen. He learned quickly to be happy just cleaning his room regularly.

Reining in Grandma

This all sounds great, Marianne. But what do I do about my mother-in-law? Or Susie, my sister who doesn't have kids and lives to buy my child every new toy that comes on the market? I hear you. People love buying gifts for kids, and I'm sure your kids are extra adorable. Recognize that these gift-buyers are probably spenders rather than savers by nature, and they enjoy shopping and buying. This is how they show love. Tread lightly.

Begin by explaining your desire that your kids always be grateful for what they have and that they never look to things for happiness or identity. Tell them you truly appreciate everything they've done in the past, but you think your children really have enough now. Offer to let them know if there's something specific your kids need. Then allow them the fun of picking it out and giving it to your children. This is a wonderful way for couples on a tight budget to get help with household expenses. I know a family whose grandparents take the kids clothes shopping twice a year. Not only is this financially practical for the family, but it also has become a very special time for grandchildren and grandparents to connect with each other.

My mother-in-law and I figured out a beautiful compromise in which I agreed to give her the idea for the gift each boy most wanted every birthday or Christmas, and she promised to not bring presents every time she visited. Deal. I don't need to be the gift superhero to my sons. I'm happy letting grandma get the tight neck hugs and the squeals of delight. I know another family who has yet to buy their own kids something for Christmas because the kids get so much from everyone else. The oldest child (age six) has yet to notice. Share this story from a mom with two kids:

> *I learned about giving my kids enough the hard way when our first child was three. We went crazy that year. We loved Christmas, and we loved our only child. We probably spent $500 on her that year. She opened presents for about 30 minutes straight. Then it was time for us to open our presents to each other. Her response? "Where's mine? The many weren't enough. Now, we do three presents with a budget of $100 per kid. I figure if three presents were enough for the King of Kings, then it's enough for our little princess and prince.*

If the gift machine can't be stopped with a friendly conversation, try offering alternatives like books, art supplies, craft sets, or other consumables. Encourage experiences that the person can do with the child like seeing a movie or ice-skating. And if stuff still comes into your home? Embrace it as reality and teach into it. "Grandma shows her love through buying things for you. Let's make sure we are always grateful and treasure each gift because it's from her. But some of these things we may keep at her house so you can play with them there. Some we may store now and take them out to play in a few months."

But We Have A Lot of People Living in Our House

A common excuse for not being able to minimize the amount of stuff is the sheer number of people living in one house. So I decided to talk to Michelle Duggar, mother of 19, to see if it was even possible to keep a house from being overrun with kids' stuff when you have that many children. I wanted to know how she coped. "Oh my, it's a real battle. We have to work diligently to keep the house organized. All the kids have to do their part too."

One way the Duggars keep the amount of stuff to a manageable level is by only buying one present for each child on their birthday and Christmas. "I usually talk to the other kids about what present would be really exciting for each child or sometimes I make up a gift basket with all kinds of treats and surprises in it." The kids don't buy birthday gifts for each other, but they do give meaningful cards and handwritten notes on birthdays. That way each child receives beautiful words of affirmation rather than 18 more presents. For Christmas they draw names so that each sibling can focus on the one person they buy for that year.

Another way this super-sized family keeps the clutter down is by rotating toys in and out of attic storage. Rather than playing with all the toys they own at once, Michelle keeps an eye on what toys are not being played with, and she moves those back up to the attic for a time. Then "new" toys come down. The family also regularly goes through toys and clothes to see if they have items that another family could use. When they receive donations from others, they take time to sort through the items and only keep those things that someone can use while giving the rest away to another family in need.

Each child has their own locker to store a limited number of special toys as well as a file box to store keepsakes. The kids add to their keepsake file over the next year or two, but they also notice what things they may no longer want to keep forever and get rid of those things before adding new ones. When Josh, the oldest, moved out to start his own family, he left with about fourteen cardboard file boxes representing his 20 years at home. If a family with 19 kids can minimize the inflow of stuff, then I bet you and I can too.

Take Action

1. Eliminate junk toys from fast food meals, dentist and doctor visits.
2. Remind your kids, "You have enough toys. These are for kids who don't yet."
3. Point out junk when you see it.
4. Gently remind the kids about past junk purchases when they consider making a new one.
5. Organize closets, rooms, drawers, and toy shelves.
6. Purge areas that have a tendency to accumulate stuff (toy boxes, bookshelves, closets).
7. Talk about plastic toy trinkets and why people like them.
8. Talk about how long the thrill of getting a new toy lasts.
9. Stay away from toy aisles and other tempting areas for a time.

CHAPTER 10

MINIMIZING THE POWER OF STUFF

Disney World. Given the subject matter of this book, the Magic Kingdom could potentially claim an entire chapter in itself. In this case it serves as the backdrop for one of the infamous "Michael Stories" that lives on in Miller Family Lore.

Disclaimer: Yes, we followed the culture to Disney World when the kids were little and camped at the Disney campground. But I'll never forget what one of the boys said after about four hours in the Magic Kingdom. He asked, "Hey, when are we going back to the campground? I want to swim and hike around." That statement, and the other boys' enthusiastic agreement, solidified our perspective about what it costs to bring happiness to our kids.

Michael was six at the time and every bit the strong-willed child God designed him to be. Early in our first day at Disney World, Michael noticed a spinning Buzz Lightyear light-up *thing* at one of the shops. The word *thing* is the only word I can think of to use, since the object held no true purpose. When you pressed a button on the side, it would light up the Buzz Lightyear as a few multi-colored plastic balls spun around and made whirling noises. It couldn't tell time or play music or, really, do anything! Despite that, it seemed as though one out of every five kids in the park had already conned their parents into purchasing one of these *things.*

Michael's love affair began with whispers to his new obsession, "Wow, those are cool." Their clandestine meetings continued throughout the day. "Hey, there's another one. That kid's got one over there!" By early evening, despite our comments about price ($12.95) and need (none), he sat with the coveted toy cradled in his arms on the floor of the gift shop. He looked up at me with tear-stained cheeks and presented his final request to consummate the relationship, "Please, can I get this?"

I bent down and tipped his chin away from Buzz and toward my face, "Do you see this toy? This toy has power over you. We are in the middle of Walt Disney World, the most amazing and fun theme park in the world, and you are sad and crying. All day we rode rides and saw cool things, but you were distracted and frustrated every time you saw this toy. You let this toy control you. You let it ruin your day." That was it. Michael, the strong-willed child, did not like it when anyone or anything had power over him. He put Buzz back on the shelf and walked out of the store.

Pointing out to your children when they are letting a toy have power over them is not fool-proof, but helping them understand this concept can serve as a strong first step in breaking free from the power of stuff. Yet before we teach this idea to our kids, we must first recognize it ourselves.

Because of my frugal upbringing, I felt certain that I was immune to the power of stuff. How could stuff control me when I kept such a watchful eye on it? But it did. More than once. When I was just getting started in the working world, I thought I needed only four pairs of shoes: brown shoes, black shoes, tennis shoes, and sandals. I seriously thought that was all anyone owned. I never noticed shoes at all—until my fashion-wise friend opened my eyes to "cute shoes." Life changing. It turns out, cute shoes were everywhere. I don't know how I'd missed them. Soon I noticed other people's cute shoes, too, since they actually owned more than four pairs.

Shortly thereafter, I learned about expensive, cute shoes. Wow, these were much gentler to my feet and would last much longer than cheap, cute shoes. After months of shopping and buying, my husband, in his infinite wisdom, finally spoke the truth that I already knew somewhere deep in my soul: There is no end to cute shoes. You must decide how many are enough.

If you find yourself in a continual cycle of pursuing the next thing you want, you may be unable to teach your children about the power of stuff until you have mastered it yourself. Figure out exactly how much time you spend shopping, researching items on the Internet, wandering through Goodwill in hopes of finding treasure, or trolling neighborhood garage sales. If the pursuit of stuff brings you an inordinate amount of pleasure, you may be letting stuff have power over *you*.

When you recognize that your child is fixating on something, ask him if he is allowing this thing to have power over him. Wanting things is OK, but obsessing over them and putting too much energy into obtaining them is a mistake with lasting effects.

Beware of Collections

Teach your kids that companies exploit this desire by offering collections of things. Why would you be satisfied with a Polar Bear Webkinz that allows you to play online with your friends when you can have the Webkinz Frog and Cat to play with also? What? They now have clothes for your pet, and you can buy a trampoline for your pet's virtual room? Well, you gotta do that! Back in the day when Beanie Babies were the rage and my mother-in-law traded them out of the trunk of her car, the Ty Company had over a 1,000 different Beanie Babies on the market, many varying only slightly with a unique smile or hair bow.

Help your child understand why companies do this (to sell more products and make more money) and how marketing strategies entice and trick (yes, use that word in your conversation) consumers into buying more than they really want and far more than they need. Buying into the lure keeps consumers dissatisfied with what they don't have rather than satisfied with what they do have. Collections keep kids on the hunt for what is new rather than enjoying what they have. Kids will likely respond with indignation because they don't like to be tricked.

At seven, Matthew began collecting Bakugans. These small balls are somehow magnetized to pop open when you roll them. Of course they come in hundreds of different shapes and sizes, and the very clever point values entice kids to keep collecting them. Despite my attempt to immunize Matthew against the Bakugan bug, he was stricken. He examined them at the store, used his allowance to buy more, and asked for them on all gift-giving occasions.

I cannot say with certainty that we triumphed over Bakugans, because he collected 38 of them before he quit. But when he finally did stop, he said with confidence, "I'm done buying Bakugans, Mom. I have enough." I did observe that once he stopped adding to his collection, he spent less time playing with the ones he already had. It turned out that these toys weren't all *that* fun in the first place. What Matthew found fun was searching for and buying new ones, not actually playing with them.

During the summer before Matthew entered middle school, he organized his closet and moved the special container of 38 Bakugans outside his door, signaling to me that these once-treasured toys now held no value to him and he wanted to get rid of them. We talked about how he desperately pursued them at age seven and then the reality of their $0 value to him at age twelve. We talked about his $120 investment in these toys and what he would do with that money if he still had it. Matthew ultimately concluded that he was glad he had bought them and also glad he stopped collecting them when he did.

Capturing these teachable moments when they occur gives us a chance to continue building a foundation for future financial decisions. Seeing a $120 investment reduced to $0 in five years might cause Matthew to rethink putting a $1,200 lift kit on a car worth only $6,000 when he's 17.

Advertising Targets

In order to effectively minimize the influence that stuff has over our children (and ourselves), we must acknowledge its power. We must realize that companies have spent huge sums of money to train us to think that this stuff is not only valuable, but also that the stuff we possess reflects our value to others.

A parent with very young children has the power to stop the love affair with stuff before in begins, but it's critical to recognize the enemy working against our best efforts. One of the reasons that stuff can wield so much power over adults and children is that marketers have delegated billions of dollars to achieve just that. In Juliet Schor's book, *Born to Buy,* she exposes the calculated methods that marketers go to in order to ensnare children's brand loyalties. Some companies donate their products to trendsetting kids to get their products to catch on in entire school systems. Because of the social influence these particular children wield, an entire classroom, grade, and ultimately an entire school can be influenced with the desire for the latest and greatest thing.[1]

Plenty of Stuff

Rarely do children in the United States ever suffer from a lack of toys. The reality is that toys are cheap, abundant and almost any household item can magically become a toy with the imagination of a child. The more common problem is too many toys. With overflowing toy boxes, bins, tubs, and shelves, it's easy to forget what a child even has. Garage sales and resale shops have contributed to the ease at which we can accumulate so many things because the cost is so low. I often have to remind myself that just because I can afford something, doesn't mean that it adds any value to our quality of life.

When our sons were really young, I took them to a garage sale or two with their allowances tightly grasped in their fists. I figured their meager allowances would go a long way at a garage sale. Unfortunately, I was all too right. We wound up owning someone else's useless stuff, including a giant pair of boxing gloves, plastic roller blades that were capable of causing permanent brain damage at a moment's notice, and an elaborate Habitrail for a gerbil that had been perfectly happy occupying a spacious aquarium.

Realizing where this train was heading, we disembarked as a family. We decided that if we truly wanted something, we would know what it was and we would save up for it or put it on a birthday or Christmas list. Desperately searching other people's garages for a hidden treasure was simply

> *The pursuit of the stuff often has even more power over our behavior than the stuff itself.*

training young children in the pursuit of the stuff. The *pursuit* of the stuff often has even more power over our behavior than the stuff itself.

After giving a financial talk one evening, a young father approached me. He wanted reassurance that his habit of going to Goodwill weekly was a good idea. He explained to me that he saved lots of money by purchasing drastically underpriced items. I challenged him to think about how many times he left the store with something that he didn't even realize he had ever wanted or needed. Or how many times did he forgo time with the family in pursuit of "good deals" on stuff that certainly could be used but wasn't missed prior to buying it? How much money would he have saved if he hadn't gone to Goodwill that week? Often a regular pursuit at thrift stores or garage sales can give stuff power over your free time and your pocketbook.

Stuff Has Power to Cause Conflicts

Have you ever noticed how often your kids fight over stuff? Does the refrain of "That's mine!" echo in your ears throughout your day? Even when hundreds of Legos are heaped on a table, isn't working together still a problem for our kids? It seems a 5-gallon tote of Hot Wheel cars is still not enough to ensure peace while racing them. This car is faster. That one is scratched. Grandma got that especially for me. He always uses that one and never lets me have a turn. The conflict seems endless.

This conflict over stuff offers the perfect opportunity to talk to kids as young as three years old about the power that stuff can have over individuals and over relationships. Take the opportunity to talk to kids about the reality that relationships with other people are what bring happiness—not stuff. Dr. David Myers, author of *Pursuit of Happiness*, identified a number of qualities shared by many people who tend to be happy.[2]

1. Happy people like themselves.
2. Happy people feel a sense of personal control.
3. Happy people are optimistic.
4. Happy people have close relationships.

Nowhere does it say that people who are happy have a lot of stuff. Teach your kids that stuff can actually pull people apart if they're not careful. When our sons were younger, I consistently removed an offending toy when it got in the way of their relationships. I gave them a chance to get along with each other while playing with the toy, but if they continued to argue, the object was removed. We cannot allow stuff to have power over our relationships.

Of course this is easier said than done. When Matthew was about four, I remember asking him in the middle of a mini-lecture, "What makes us happy? People or things? You know this, buddy."

Without missing a beat, he said, "Actually Mom, people who buy me things make me really happy!"

A Possible Addiction?

In Gloria DeGaetano's book, *Parenting Well in a Media Age*, the author writes of a behavior that has been observed in experiments done with rats. When rats are placed in a laboratory setup with an electrode attached to the pleasure center of their brains, and are given a choice to press a button that will give them food or one that will simply stimulate the pleasure center in their brains, many rats will end up starving themselves to death by consistently choosing the experience of pleasure over food. This constrained choice conditions an addictive response that separates the rat from awareness of its own real life needs.[3]

The acquisition of stuff can be a powerful motivator to pursue even more stuff. For many kids and adults alike, buying things produces good feelings. Jane Velez-Mitchell, in her book *Addict Nation: An Intervention for America*, parallels compulsive shopping with other addictions. She writes that like all addicts, the shoppers need to increase their purchases to get the same "high" that they got at the beginning. Also, for those who are truly addicted, not shopping actually produces symptoms of withdrawal.[4]

Michael has grown from the child on the floor of the Disney World gift shop into a young man who can research an item when necessary and wait patiently until he is sure that he wants something. He still finds great joy when he decides to spend his money, but he's no longer captivated by the allure of "the next thing."

One evening when he was about fourteen, I walked into the room where he was on the computer. He very quickly closed out what he'd been looking at with a look of guilt and left the room. Uh oh, I thought. A quick check of the history showed that he had been . . . shopping for air soft guns (realistic-looking guns that shoot plastic BBs). Twelve different sites with hundreds of different guns. Obviously, he thought we would be upset if we caught him shopping online.

The next day I sat down with him to discuss his progress from the days of Buzz Lightyear. Researching an item and shopping around for competitive pricing were valuable tools for making wise financial decisions. I praised him for going a year being happy with the gun he had. I reviewed the reasoning he used to decide that he might need another gun because, "A P-9 pistol is one you can use in a battle that is easy to get to for close shots. It's good in night battles because you don't want to slam your bigger gun into a tree in the dark. I found a great deal on the Air Soft GI website." Okay, Michael, you had me at hello.

Helping him understand himself and the very real power of stuff enabled him to curb his once insatiable appetite for more. Over time his need to spend has diminished and his financial filter has become more developed. He also now has a keen sense of when things might have power over one of his brothers or even one of his parents. As my husband updated the family on the arrival of the new iPhone, Michael commented, "Are you sure this phone isn't having power over you, Dad?" It's good to have accountability.

CHAPTER 11

THE BEAUTY OF DELAYED GRATIFICATION

At age 14, Bryan decided he wanted to buy a bike. Not just a regular bike but a real cycling store $1,200 Trek mountain bike. He had already earned a couple hundred dollars before the summer even started by spreading mulch and preparing garden beds for a handful of neighbors. Now with his $1,200 goal in site, he amped up his marketing and found a few more neighbors who had plenty of odd jobs for the summer. By September, he had reached his goal.

After a few more weeks of test driving bikes, researching on the Trek website, and negotiating pricing at different bike stores, Bryan announced he wasn't buying a bike. He thought $1,200 was quite a lot of money. It took him an entire summer to earn that much. As fall approached, he realized that in Indiana a bike is really only useable for a little over half of the year, which made a $1,200 bike not a great value in his mind. After another month of thinking and researching, he bought a Mac Book Air with his money instead.

By delaying the purchase of the bike, he was able to make a thoughtful decision. Plus, he appreciated the value of the computer. But this is not the cultural norm. The message of the culture is *Buy now, pay later! You deserve a break today! Get it now while supplies last! Sign up early so you won't be disappointed*! But is waiting actually the better way to go?

Stanford University conducted the well-known marshmallow test to discover the implications for children who were able to delay gratification. This study followed participants over two decades to conclude that those children who were able to delay eating a treat were more successful as adults than the children who couldn't wait. During the initial testing, a marshmallow or other favorite treat was set before children ages 4-6. They were told that if they sat for 15 minutes without eating, they would be given more treats. Those children who were able to wait to eat the treat displayed many successful traits later in life, including scoring higher on the SAT test than the children who couldn't wait.[1]

When my two older boys were young, I read about this study and was curious if my sons would be able to delay gratification. Andy and I used M&Ms since they coveted those the most. We gave them each four M&Ms and told them that if they did not eat any of them for fifteen minutes they would get eight more—a 200% return on their time investment. The boys sat at a table and stared at their candies. When we returned to the room, Bryan sat contently with his four colorful candies while Michael sat sheepishly in front of four white M&Ms. He had licked them all and then put them back in place, so that technically he did not *eat* the candies. Despite Michael's initial struggles with delaying gratification, he did mature into a successful student and responsible teen, albeit one who still will eat an entire package of M&Ms in minutes.

If we know it is good for kids to wait, why do we sometimes feel guilty for depriving our children of their immediate desires? Some parents fear their children's sadness or anger. Others feel they are not fulfilling their role as parent if they do not provide those things they can afford to buy. But if we block out the messages of the culture, we know in our hearts that we should be saying "no" more.

Just Say No

As the parent, you do know what's best. You know that kids' appetites for stuff are insatiable. You know that whatever it is they want, it will not make them happy for very long. You know that what the child really needs is more of you and less stuff. You know that buying it offers you the easy way out of the store, but that it only conditions them to ask again next time.

We must "just say no." It's short and simple and to the point. Say it with the same confidence you would use if they asked you, "Can I throw this aerosol can in the fire?" If you have randomly said yes in the past to goodies from the store, then your child will have a lot more motivation to plead his case. At this point, he still has hope that it might pay off to badger; therefore, it may take more time for him to recognize the word "no" in your vocabulary. He may need to be physically removed from the coveted object, or perhaps even the store itself. Don't repeat the word "no." Just leave. Have no fear— this will only be a temporary situation while the child becomes acquainted with the new sheriff in town.

Variations of "no" that won't work:

Rather than a firm "no," some parents prefer the weaker version of "We can't afford that now."
This is simply not true. If you have a credit card in your wallet, then you probably could buy every toy in whatever aisle you're standing in. You could buy boxes of Hershey bars and every flavor of bubble gum. And then you would simply return home to the Visa bill in the mailbox, having incurred a little more debt for the family. Give your child the security of knowing that you *could* buy the object, but that it is not part of your family's plan for your money.

"Maybe later," "Not today," or "I need to think about that."
All of these responses delay the problem for another day. These answers give them hope that perhaps the conditions just weren't right for their request to be granted, but *next* time they might have success. These responses work to put them off in the moment, but they fail to present your stance on the acquisition of stuff. The subtle message is that you wish you could buy it, but for some reason unbeknownst to them, you just can't right then.

"That's too expensive. Pick out something else."
According to my local toy store owner, the term "Shut-up Toys" is used in the toy boutique industry to refer to the low-priced toys placed seductively around the cash register at a child's eye-level. These trinkets serve as lifeboats for parents who want to say yes to their child but cannot afford the desired item. They said no to the large ticket item so buying something smaller seems harmless. However, that lifeboat has a hole in it, because it actually rewards the child with stuff, which feeds the appetite for more next time. The child has indeed "shut-up," but they have been encouraged to scream on another day.

Variations of "no" that will work

"Do you want to put it on your list?"
As we discussed earlier, each family member should keep his or her own list for optional purchases. Doing so cultivates financial discernment, allowing for thoughtful purchases rather than impulsive ones. Asking the child this question allows them to consider if the item is even worthy enough to be put on the list. Many times when I have asked one of my boys this question, he has looked at the object more closely and then said, "No, never mind." Which means, "I can't believe I even asked because this thing's not even worth taking the

time to write down." For a time, one of the boys had "an ice pick" on his list. (He scratched it off 15 days later.)

"Have you saved enough of your allowance for that?"
Once you've explained to your child that you will provide them with everything they need and even some of what they want, the allowance (See Chapter 13) is the perfect way for children to provide for themselves things they really want. Very quickly, parents see that it is much easier for children to spend their parents' money rather than their own.

"Would you like to hold this while I shop and then give it back?"
This variation was an all-time favorite of mine when my sons were still young enough to sit in the shopping cart seat. I admitted to the allure of the object and used its powers to my benefit. The child would be absorbed in the newness of the object and all the fascination it possessed, which allowed me to shop without disturbance. Not once did any of them throw a fit when it was time to return it to the shelf because they never believed it was in the realm of possibility that a toy could be bought for no reason.

~∞∞∞~

But kids don't want to hear "no." They don't want to wait. When Roald Dahl's Veruca Salt shouted the infamous, "I want it *now*, Daddy!" she had no intention of delaying her desires. But how often do our desires change if we wait? How much more do we appreciate the item or experience if we waited for it? How much stronger do we feel if we don't allow our desires to control us?

Bryan waited to buy his expensive bike, and that worked well for him. But that was not always how he operated. When

> *How much more do we appreciate the item or experience if we waited for it?*

he started middle school, pimple-faced and insecure, he was less sure of who he was and what he wanted. At the start of 6th grade, the school sent home an order form for spirit wear. The form included an array of sweatshirts, t-shirts, shorts, socks, and bandanas that would display the student's school spirit to the world. Bryan came home and asked me for a new sweatshirt.

"Oh, do you need another sweatshirt? Because these don't seem like a very good deal." We looked through his dresser drawers together, and it seemed like he had at least five or six sweatshirts that fit him and looked in great shape. "It doesn't seem like you need a new sweatshirt. Do you have your own money to buy it?" A bit of whining occurred followed shortly thereafter by the comparison card, "Other kids at school just take home this form, and their parents send in the money. It's not that difficult."

Since he was more than ready to spend my money and not at all interested in spending his own, I continued to push back on the idea of yet another sweatshirt. His hormones raged. My resolve strengthened. And finally the explosion occurred. Red faced and teary-eyed he announced, "I am *sick* of you guys pretending we're *poor!*"

I snapped. That's not at all what we were doing. I was furious. Didn't he realize we had deliberately chosen to teach him all these things so that he could be a financially secure adult? Didn't he know that we wanted him to never find his identity in the clothes he wore or the stuff he owned? Couldn't he see that this was for his own good? Much to my chagrin, I grabbed his elbow and pulled him back to my bedroom closet where I removed from my top shelf the *exact* sweatshirt he'd asked for. At back-to-school registration I had seen the sweatshirt and known he would like it, so I had already bought it for his upcoming birthday.

Shaking the sweatshirt in front of him I furthered my rant, "Are you happy now? I bought this for your birthday!"

He looked at the sweatshirt, then at me, then back to the sweatshirt. With tears still descending he countered, "Now you ruined my birthday!"

This was not one of my finer parenting moments. But it does clearly depict how frustrated Bryan got when being forced to delay gratification and how excited he expected to be when receiving new surprises on his birthday. He and I talked about the excitement of getting new things, especially things we've been wanting for a long time. We talked about the culture at school that influenced his perception that spirit wear was one of his basic human rights. And we talked about contentment and gratitude and how these two attitudes can add so much joy to our lives.

Taming the Terror at Target

We can easily teach kids to delay gratification in daily life. It's not uncommon for parents to avoid taking their children to the store with them because they don't want to deal with the barrage of requests. But stores offer a prime training ground. And how much more freedom will parents feel if they are able to get their personal tasks completed with their children accompanying them, rather than having to work around leaving them at home with a sitter?

I had happily shopped with my four boys without incident for months until a warm day in June of 2009. That day, I realized my radar had failed to pick up the storm clouds I should have seen brewing. Six-year-old Matthew asked his big brother, "Michael, what are you going to buy me today?"

Michael innocently responded, "Oh Matthew, I don't have any money with me today." As if on cue, Matthew dropped to the ground and shrieked, then convulsed in a heap of anger, frustration, and disbelief. I suddenly caught on to what had been happening over the last month. Michael, a spender by nature, had been getting a lot of joy from buying his younger brother little treats at Target. A pack of Juicy Fruit here, a box of Gobstoppers there. Not every trip, but enough to create an expectation.

I stood over Matthew's sobbing body and asked the other boys to gather around. "Do you see this? Do you understand what this is? Do you know how this happened?" Michael bowed his head with the reality of the situation. "This! This is why I never bought you guys stuff when you were little. This is a boy who used to be happy when we shopped. This is a boy who is miserable because of stuff." Matthew eventually stood up, dusted himself off, and moved on. But after that day, Michael started giving his brother extra cool birthday and Christmas presents and a random surprise rather than regular little treats at Target.

If your children are still young enough or sheltered enough to not beg for "the stuff," be sure you continue to be in charge of what gets placed in your shopping cart. By never starting the habit of buying a "treat" or worse yet "a surprise if you're good," you can ensure a minimally disruptive trip to the store. Of course many parents have used the goodies at the store to motivate good behavior, and no child will spontaneously transform into a spoiled brat upon the offering of a treat. I even carried that parenting tool in my tool belt, until I thought more about it and saw the bad habits it was creating.

Bribing and rewarding kids with a treat for obedient behavior at the store causes problems in two areas. First, bribing for good behavior conditions children that they should get a treat every time your family enters a store. Like Pavlov's dog, some kids begin to salivate when the automatic doors open. They begin to expect the treat. Denial of the treat for any reason is like pressing the "fit-throwing button." Second, bribing minimizes your parental role, reducing you to a dispenser of rewards and punishments. Kids should "be good" at the store simply because that's what you asked them to do. It's the right thing to do. Pleasing you and respecting your authority should be their motivation rather than what reward they'll get.

When children don't expect toys or treats, you enjoy the added bonus of peaceful shopping on top of the joy of giving abundance. Because you have done your homework and said no with regularity, you are in a position to give your kids a real treat. About every month or so, I'll buy the kids a giant Icee to split with a brother or open a box of ice cream bars that I just bought. "Wow, Mom! Thanks. This is awesome!" They are thrilled with something as simple as half of an Icee or a 25 cent ice cream sandwich.

Certainly, they've accused me of being mean mom, stingy mom, and unfair mom. But when I'm able to make kids so happy that they literally squeal with joy over a treat that costs less than one dollar, I feel like super mom, rock-star mom, and the best-mom-in-the-world mom.

Practice Shopping

If you've started this book and realize that you've already started creating habits that are making it difficult for your children to be grateful for what they have, don't condemn yourself for yesterday. You can begin today. You can sit your children down today and tell them, "I've noticed it's difficult for us to go into a store and have a pleasant experience. This isn't good for you or me, and it won't serve you well as an adult."

During a season when our boys had started slacking in their ability to get through a store without difficulty, Andy and I set aside a weekend to practice shopping. Rather than going the easier route, which would be leaving them home, we decided to practice the desired behavior. Taking your children with you to do mundane tasks is important to your freedom, and it's important for teaching them to be knowledgeable consumers and patient children.

Early one Saturday morning we explained to the boys that taking them into stores with us had become an unpleasant experience. We told them they must need more practice shopping in order to master it. As athletes, they practice basketball. As students, they practice handwriting. As our children, they needed to practice shopping. After outlining both appropriate and inappropriate behavior, we proceeded to run errands. We explained we had enough errands to last all day and on to the next if it took them that long to catch on. They caught on. After visiting four stores, including the ever-challenging JoAnn Fabrics, we declared the morning a success and reminded them that we would be watching to see when they might need another practice session.

Relationships Matter More than the Stuff

Start saying "no" to demands for stuff and start saying "yes" to making special time to connect with them when they are not asking for it. Pull up a chair and really listen to what happened during school that day, or snuggle with them before bed and listen as they relate the highs and lows of their day. Substituting time for stuff will make the transition away from the stuff much easier.

When contemplating appropriate times to connect, I suggest finding times when your children are *not* demanding your attention. First, if you only connect when your kids are seeking attention and/or whining, you have added to their entitlement. They whine, "I'm bored. I want you to play a game with me." So you stop making dinner and begrudgingly play with them, surreptitiously cheating so the game will end sooner. Connecting like this can send the message that you played with them only because they demanded it—kids learn quickly how to read our lack of enthusiasm.

Of course, you can always stop what you're doing to play with them, but if you do, first be sure you send the message that it was your idea: "That would be great! I was just thinking about wanting to take a break and play a game with you." Second, being preemptive with attention—showering it on them when they are not asking for it—helps them feel valued and special. It sends them the message that you want to connect with them and you find them valuable, as opposed to responding simply because they whined and you caved.

Similarly, if you do want to buy them something for no specific occasion, like a new puzzle, bubbles, a pool toy, or a book, either tell them you need their help to pick it out before you go in to the store, or buy it secretly and give it to them at home as a surprise. As long as you remain in charge and don't allow yourself to be manipulated by your child's desires, they will quickly learn to be grateful for everything that you do buy them.

Houston, We Have a Problem

The slow creep into entitlement and ingratitude can also come about after you have trained your children to be grateful. I realized not long ago that my youngest son, Matthew, at age eleven, was feeling entitled to certain experiences. While on vacation at a beautiful beach for a day of playing in the ocean he announced, "This is so boring. Is this all that we are going to do all day? Can't we rent a paddleboat or something?" Wait a minute. He was no longer content at a beach on the ocean? Shells and water and sand were no longer enough? He needed to spend $50 to paddle around in a plastic boat?

I realized that we had grown complacent in monitoring his experiences. The older boys were grateful, so we had started to do more activities as they grew older. They continued to appreciate every one of them. Matthew, as a younger child, had begun to expect these things and finally arrived at a place where the beach was "boring."

Needless to say, we did not rent a boat that day. In fact, after a conversation about entitlement and discontentment, we cut back on extra activities and experiences until we saw his joy in the simple things in life return. If we had rented the boat, we would have appeased his boredom for the moment, but we would have set him on a path to be unhappy and discontent unless he was being entertained.

Delaying gratification is a powerful skill to master. By putting off what we immediately want, we are less controlled by our impulses. If a child feels hungry but learns to wait without complaining until food is available, he learns that he is not controlled by his hunger. He learns that feeling hungry does not have to make him miserable. If a child needs help with homework but learns to wait until Mom is finished in the kitchen, he learns that other people have lives apart from his. He learns to be grateful when Mom does put down her project to help him with his. If a child wants a toy but is told to wait, he often learns that he doesn't really want the toy very much since he soon forgets why it was so attractive in the first place.

How can we model delaying gratification for our children? One way to allow the kids to see Andy and me delay gratification is to talk as a family about financial decisions we are considering. Should we put in a garden this year? What would the costs be? Should we replace the roof or just fix it? Even when the boys were younger, we let them overhear us making decisions and putting things on our own list.

If children rarely wait for things they want, they're robbed of the opportunity to experience deep gratitude for the object. If they never hear "no" or "not right now" or "put it on your list," they miss an opportunity to develop their financial filter. But if they learn to wait, if they learn to be content with what they have, they will grow into adults who can easily manage any income with confidence and peace.

Chapter 12

PREPARING THEM
FOR POVERTY

A summer triathlon sounded like a great idea when I signed up in April. After all, I had three months to train and prepare my body and mind. I already knew how to swim, I owned a bike, and, if chased, I could run pretty fast. How difficult could it be? Needless to say, my great *intentions* to train did not help me do well in the race. Passing an elderly woman in the last 100 yards—so I wouldn't come in dead last—isn't something to brag about. It turns out that actually training and preparing several months *before* the race would have ensured a more successful finish.

Likewise, we do our kids a disservice if we do not train them purposefully for living their lives independently from us. **Yet many parents not only fail to train, they actually create lifestyles for their families that are not financially feasible or sustainable and cannot be duplicated until decades after the kids leave home—a fact many parents forget to tell their children.**

A Skewed Standard

How often have you heard kids complain about being poor? Frequently parents lament in front of their children about how they wish they were rich. They share dreams of exotic vacations, fancy cars or even winning the lottery. But very few Americans would *not* fall into the "wealthy" category, on a worldwide scale. The definition of poor is "lacking sufficient money to live at a standard considered comfortable or normal in a society." Since the 1980s when credit cards began to flourish as a way to subsidize incomes, fewer people actually had to settle for the lifestyle their incomes dictated. Rather, they just needed to convince a credit card company to loan them money so they could buy the stuff that would help them feel comfortable and normal in their culture. The "stuff" was cloaked as "emergencies" because they'd already spent the money for predictable expenses (like home maintenance and car repairs) on the "stuff," making it unavailable when the "emergency" happened.

Because we tend to compare ourselves with others who have more stuff than we do, we are left feeling "poor." Consider the second grader who doesn't have a cool enough bike, or the middle schooler without a cell phone, or the high schooler without a car. They all *feel* poor. But they, and we, are not poor. Not compared to the rest of the world.

While they still live at home, teach your kids that your family is rich. Over half the world does not have a refrigerator. Almost half the world lives on $2.50 a day or less.[1] Visit globalrichlist. com. Within minutes, you can calculate that you or your child is the _____ richest person in the world. For example, my 17-year-old son earned about $3,000 last year putting him in the top 31.39%; he would be the 1,883,349,739th richest person in the world.[2]

From the time they're toddlers, children absorb all the subtle messages you send out each day so be purposeful in your words, actions, and attitudes about money and possessions. Be sure to consistently communicate that your family has been blessed with many financial resources, as well as the ability to live in a country where working hard is rewarded. Tell them that since you have been given much, much is then expected. Luke writes in his Gospel, "From everyone who has been given much, much will be demanded; and from the one who has been entrusted with much, much more will be asked" (Luke 12:48). Kids at all income levels have a responsibility to manage their resources wisely.

We have the power to feel grateful for what we've been given or discontent about what we do not have. When kids ask about a Florida vacation, we have the power to tell them, "Right now, we don't have money budgeted for that, but we can go camping with your cousins next weekend." If we approach the family's finances in a matter-of-fact way, our kids will be more likely to accept God's provision and our active role in being wise stewards.

> *We have the power to feel grateful for what we've been given or discontent about what we do not have.*

The Insidious Influence of Culture

If we parented our kids in a bubble, it would be quite simple to get this message across. But we don't. We have to navigate life in materialistic 21st century America. And it's not always easy. I'll never forget the story one mom told me about moving her family from the inner city to the suburbs.

For ten years, they had raised two daughters in a 1,800-square foot house in a downtown Indianapolis neighborhood. The girls shared a bedroom, but they never really complained since most of the other kids in the neighborhood did the same thing. With the cultural norm that "all families move to a bigger house once they can afford it" firmly planted in their minds, the family was finally able to move into a four-bedroom house in a new suburban neighborhood. The girls were ecstatic.

On move-in day the mom recalled, "They were running around singing and dancing in and out of each room. They were elated to each have their own room, as well as a family room and a living room. They kept singing to each other about how huge the new house was."

That excitement lasted three weeks—until the 10-year-old had a new friend from school over. "Where is your guys' basement? Why don't you have a basement to play in?" That's all it took. The oldest daughter now questioned, "Why didn't we get a house with a basement?" The gratitude for the new, larger home was quickly replaced with discontentment.

A mom who was a missionary from Brazil told a similar story. "When we are on the mission field my kids are perfectly content to have a refrigerator the size of a dorm fridge and no dryer for clothes. We rarely keep more than two or three days' worth of food in the house, and they each have only one drawer full of clothes. When we are back in the States for a visit, this changes within a week. They compare themselves with their neighborhood friends and whine and complain about the things they don't have."

Teach solid, biblical truths to your kids at a young age. Do they want to feel poor based on how others are living? Or do they want to feel rich based on the blessings God has given them? They will technically be "poor" when they first leave your house. And that's OK. In God's economy, contentment makes a poor person feel rich while discontentment makes a rich person feel poor. The specific amount of money and possessions matters much less than our attitude about the money and possessions.

Even the affluent suffer from feeling poor because of the influence of television. Consider this: 1954 was the last year that most Americans rated themselves as "very happy" in a national poll.[3] Shortly after 1954, the popularity of television sets in American homes increased drastically. Coincidence? I don't think so. Certainly, commercials give us opportunities to see more and more things we don't have and might possibly need, but the television shows themselves give us an opportunity to see how other people are living. Our kids now think it's normal to have a playroom off their bedrooms, elaborate wardrobes in their closets, and a pool in their backyard.

Setting Realistic Expectations

If being poor means lacking the money to live up to the comfortable standards of the culture, so what? Who cares if our kids leave our house and live below the standards of the culture? If they leave expecting to be poor, but they have a solid plan for making financial progress over time, then can't we inspire them to embrace their limited time with a perceived, "limited" financial status? Dave Ramsey, radio host and author of *Total Money Makeover*, boldly inspires this same concept with his call to, "Live like no one else, so you can live like no one else."[4]

From the time my boys were young, we have regaled them with stories of "our poor years"—days when we scrounged the car for change so that we could rent a movie and we ate pasta every night, simply changing the shape of the noodle. For our first Christmas, I bought Andy a white shirt, and he bought me a stuffed animal I still cherish. Twenty-five years later, I can't remember what we got each other last Christmas.

We have told the boys about our milk crate furniture, threadbare carpet, and noisy apartment where we could hear our neighbor upstairs using the bathroom at night. With these stories and countless others planted deeply in their brains, our teenage sons have begun to stockpile household goods and furniture that they retrieved from our Goodwill pile.

If your kids are currently living a fairly carefree life, enjoying all the things that you worked to provide over the years, they may need to be reminded that this is not how they will start out their life as an adult. Not preparing our kids for poverty is like training them for a rigorous hike on the Appalachian Trail, but then failing to give them a pack with supplies. They will do well for a little while, but pretty soon they're going to need food, water, and shelter. A pack brimming with supplies would be life-giving after six hours on the trail.

I distinctly remember counseling a couple in their mid-twenties. A mere two years into marriage, they already carried a high credit card debt load as well as two large car payments each month. When we talked to them about getting rid of the more expensive car and saving up cash for a much cheaper one, the young man looked defeated. He lowered his head, wrung his hands and told us, "When I was sixteen, I drove a nicer car than the one I will be buying now. I feel like I am going backwards." He was.

But your children don't have to. If you choose to have an extra car in the family for your children to drive, consider calling it *your* car. Some parents I know have even worked out deals for their working high schooler to lease the family car for a reasonable amount each month. Consider this the perfect opportunity to teach your kids about license and registration fees, oil changes, gas, and general maintenance. We are not being loving to our kids when we miss this opportunity to put them on a solid foundation. The sweet sixteen car with the big bow on it sure looks exciting at the time, but what about when Darling Daughter is 23, the car is nine years old, and she's on her own financially? Will that car be a blessing or a curse?

Some teenagers want to buy their own cars with their own money. While this is a noble idea, what if that desire was delayed? Perhaps the teen could borrow your car instead and continue growing their savings account so when they're out on their own, they could pay cash for a car. If they could save $2,500, they could buy an older car that could last at least a year or two without major repairs. During that year or two, they could make "car payments" to themselves. That way, when they were ready for a "new-to-them" car, they would have cash in the bank to buy a nicer car. Plus, the older car would still have some value remaining for the trade.

This entire plan is impossible, though, if the young adult considers an older car "embarrassing to drive." One of our most challenging counseling cases was with a middle-aged business manager who had a $675 car payment each month. This payment caused the family to barely make it until the next paycheck. We convinced him to get rid of the car and pay cash for a low-end, used Toyota. He did this for six months before he was simply too frustrated by the fact that people who worked for him drove nicer cars than he did. He sold the Toyota and bought something more prestigious. And the bonds of debt got a little tighter.

While they are under your roof, your kids must learn that the car they drive doesn't impact their identity. Who they are as people is not dictated by the value of their car or any other possessions. Yes, TV ads attempt to sell that message, but we have more power than they do. We can counter these messages by watching commercials together with our children and talking to them about the marketing techniques companies use. We can also model not being impressed by someone based on the car they drive. When we send the subtle message that "The neighbors must be doing well" because they just bought a high-priced car, we teach our kids that a fancy car indicates success. It does not.

Besides nice cars, kids must also understand that vacations, frequent eating out, and nice homes do not automatically accompany their first real job offer, despite the fact that it seems like they are finally making "all the money in the world." As they get closer and closer to their launch from your home to theirs, help them establish lower expectations about how they will live. "Mom and Dad have been earning money for decades, and we have been wise with our spending. If you want to live unhindered by debt, you need to realize you will not have extra money for the things we do now." Share their launch with a sense of adventure rather than doom. If you do, you'll send them on this journey with an understanding that many kids won't have.

> *Share their launch with a sense of adventure rather than doom.*

Shaping First Paycheck Experiences

Prior to getting their first real job after their schooling is complete, most kids have had some experience earning money working during the summers or working part-time jobs during high school or college. Babysitting, lawn mowing, and yard work also give kids great first experiences with their own money. As parents, it is our role to strategically shape these initial experiences so that they can prove beneficial to our kids rather than destructive.

Frequently, kids ages twelve and thirteen earn money from babysitting. In the past, the hourly rate was well below the minimum wage for that time. When I babysat in middle school, minimum wage was $3.35 and I earned $2.00/hour babysitting for a family with two young children. All my friends earned the same rate, and we were quite pleased with it. My babysitting money allowed me the perfect opportunity to learn to give to the needy, save for the future, and spend a few dollars to go to the movies once a month.

Presently, teens earn in the range of $8-$10 per hour for doing the same job I did. Such skyrocketing wages may be the result of fewer teens being interested in earning money since their parents meet all their financial needs. With fewer workers available, many families with young children feel compelled to woo the preteen out of their homes and into the babysitting work force with a higher wage. Or, perhaps the shortage of teens interested in working relates to the fact that sports teams have become so all consuming.

Whatever the reason for these excessive wages, many grown men trying to support their families earn only about $8.00 an hour in physically taxing jobs. If preteens and young teens can demand such incredibly high hourly rates and are allowed the freedom to spend this money however they want, their young financial minds develop gross misconceptions about true earning potential. This can cement bad habits. Statistics show that, on average, teens spend 98% of their income.[5] Since they probably aren't paying to heat their rooms or to eat three meals a day, they can spend this money on whatever they happen to want at any given time. This dangerous habit lays the groundwork for future, reckless spending.

So what can parents do to counteract cultural influences? **For starters, encourage—or even require—them to get jobs.** Set expectations that they've reached the age where they should earn their own money. Point out that babysitting and yard work are good options available to them. Then explain the problems that can result from earning too high of an income (unrealistic expectations, future job frustration…), and insist they charge a wage lower than minimum wage. This saves young families money at a time when many need the help. It also saves the young teen from any of the negative effects of high pay for fairly easy work.

A friend of mine had no idea what families paid for babysitters. So when her 13-year-old daughter returned home with a $20 bill after only two hours of babysitting a sleeping baby, this mom was shocked. Without hesitation, she explained to her daughter that $10.00 an hour was too much, and she called to ask the family to accept half of it back or receive two more hours of babysitting for free. Granted, some families want to show their appreciation to a young teen for their services, but as a regular occurrence, the situation will create a false sense of financial reality that will rarely be duplicated. Just imagine: $10.00 an hour—watch TV—no taxes— no expenses. Sign me up.

When my second son turned fourteen, he begged us to let him get a summer job at a local country club as a caddy. After much thought and prayer, Andy and I both decided that Bryan was not old enough to be in a situation where he could be excessively tipped (rumors of $100 tips) and where adults were frequently very casual with money, often betting on various aspects of their games. We didn't want this for his first real job. Once he turned sixteen and had already experienced working hard for minimal pay, then being a caddy might certainly be a positive experience.

Even a minimum wage job at the local grocery store should be leveraged to provide as much training for the future as possible. Discuss with your child how much of their paycheck will be put back for their college expenses or their post college expenses. Decide how much they should give away from each paycheck. What other expenses will the job create—extra gas to get there or additions to their wardrobe?

Getting kids excited about putting a chunk of their hard earned money in the bank is not as difficult as you might first think. Rather than having them feel like you are *taking* their money, help them understand they are actually *giving* the money to their future selves. The money will be available for them. Remind them of all the well-educated and high income-producing people who have squandered their money and whose net worth is negative even after decades of income. Starting at a young age with "money in the bank" is a habit that will help ensure a strong start and ultimately a more successful financial journey.

But few kids can get money in the bank because fewer and fewer teens pursue summer jobs or even part-time jobs. Why is this the case? One reason is sports. No longer a hobby or something kids do for a little fun, organized sports have become some kids' "job." With practices, games, private coaching, travel tournaments, and summer camps, many young athletes literally have no time to hold down a part-time job. Coaches now demand this type of commitment, and they can get it. Parents are drawn to what the sports can teach their kids, but they are also drawn to the hope of a scholarship.

Despite this norm, I would encourage all parents to prioritize giving their children the opportunity to earn money outside the home. Having a boss, learning to be on time, doing challenging and even boring tasks are all experiences kids should have prior to getting their first job as an adult.

We must prepare our kids for life outside our homes. We must walk alongside them as they grow and mature, gently nudging them with the reality that awaits them after they leave our homes. While I love the thought of creating a well-feathered nest, I need to remind myself regularly that they will leave this nest and build their own someday. Preparing them for poverty will enable them to leave our family well equipped for the adventure that awaits.

CHAPTER 13

THE POWER AND PITFALLS OF THE ALLOWANCE

You can start preparing your kids for their own financial futures at a very young age. Giving kids their own money to manage provides an excellent way to provide them with early experiences handling money. When is a child ready? When you hear these coming out of their mouth:

- "Can you buy me that?"
- "Hey, that's cool."
- "Can I get it?"
- "I want one!"

These are the "sounds" of a child who's ready for an allowance. Parents must determine when to begin an allowance. When the maturity of each child coincides with the child's desire for money and the things money can buy, it's time to think about giving your child an allowance. Most of my boys started getting an allowance around age five. This was the age when they started asking for slushies at Target and gum from the gas station. They had also reached the age where they were mature enough to start helping out around the house.

Though some would say no child really needs an allowance, I have found that giving a child some spending money provides a valuable opportunity to teach financial principles that are best learned by kids who have access to their own money.

The Power of Chores

We started chores at the same time we started allowances. Maturity is necessary because remembering to do extra chores around the house will take some effort. Children need regular training, guidance and accountability once we require them to take on extra tasks. We explained the allowance money as "the money from our family budget that we would have spent on you, but now you are old enough to decide what you want to do with it." The chores started at the same time because, "If you are old enough to get an allowance, then you are old enough for chores."

Andy and I defined chores as those jobs you do to help out simply because you are part of the family. Chores help Mom and Dad with the collective job of running the household. Making beds, cleaning rooms, and clearing dinner plates are considered personal responsibilities rather than chores because those tasks are simply the child taking care of the child. While there is no one way to manage chores and allowances, a few underlying principles should apply. Parents should "market" chores as something kids and parents do to contribute to the overall running of the household. They aren't a punishment or something to moan and groan about. "You are now old enough to share some of the responsibilities around the house with Mom and Dad."

Parents must understand that children who do chores gain satisfaction from their effort. They feel like contributors to the household. They feel important. Consider children who live on farms or children from only a few generations ago whose parents needed them to start helping out as soon as they were physically able. These kids matured faster and had more confidence in their abilities. Yet today some parents feel guilty for giving their child work, or worse yet, some parents feel like it's not worth the battle to ensure the chores are completed.

Kids must learn to help around the house. This is good for them—even if they don't agree. Not only will they feel more self-confident in general, they will also be skilled in the very tasks that all adults need to learn to navigate. It doesn't make sense to insist on French and geometry (which only a few may use in the future) but ignore cleaning, organizing, and completing home repairs (things they'll all need to do one day).

Mystified as to where to start with possible chores? Here's a list to get you started:

Preschool:

- Empty silverware from dishwasher
- Set the table
- Put away 10 things around the house
- Wipe baseboards
- Dust all the corners in the house with a high duster
- Wipe fingerprints off doors/windows
- Organize the pantry
- Sort laundry
- Match socks

Elementary Age:

- Vacuum
- Feed/walk/clean up after pets
- Put away groceries
- Empty trash
- Dust
- Help make dinner

- Water plants
- Load and unload dishwasher
- Put away seasonal decorations
- Mop
- Help with gardening
- Wipe counter tops
- Clean the bathroom
- Sweep out the garage
- Rake leaves/shovel snow

Teens:

- Do household repairs (Caulk, painting, drywall,)
- Prepare full meals
- Clean up the entire kitchen after a meal
- Clean/organize the garage
- Help with lawn maintenance (mulching, planting/trimming flowers/trees, edging)
- Master all of the chores listed above

Consider the big picture and that some of these chores might actually be helpful while others might simply serve to teach the child a skill that could take some time to perfect.

Though some experts recommend directly linking chores to the allowance, I've found it easier to keep them separate, though they may begin at the same time. These authors suggest that if a child doesn't complete their chores, they don't get their full allowance. This makes sense and certainly would work. But practically speaking, I never felt like being the chore police—tracking my kids' every movement with charts as to who would be paid what amount and for which chores. Also, keep in mind that many kids would rather skip the chore and skip the money at times. Since I want my children to have access to money, keeping the allowance separate from chore completion made the most sense for our family.

If a child can't manage to get their chores finished without a lot of reminding or without a sour attitude, then this is a discipline issue. Our rule is that the boys must completely finish their chores by noon on Saturday or my husband and I double what's required of them. Plus, the child cannot leave the house until all chores are finished. So if each child had seven chores for the week and one of the boys leaves two chores unfinished at noon on Saturday, then that child has four more chores to do (2+2) before leaving the house. If the completion of chores becomes a regular problem, then allowance stops—and so will chores—until the child is "more responsible." With more responsibilities come more privileges. Fewer responsibilities mean fewer privileges.

The actual amount of the allowance must be low, about enough to buy a few food treats a week or enough to save for a month for a new book or small toy. Because the allowance amount is low, extra jobs provide a great opportunity to learn a good work ethic and earn extra money. A "job" is different than a chore in that it is beyond the ordinary work (maintenance-type chores that keep the household running) they do, and it is contracted out at either a specific hourly rate or an agreed amount for the completed job. This is where the fun happens.

> *We cannot provide our children with everything they want or they will have no motivation whatsoever to work to earn money.*

Jobs usually originate when a child needs extra money for something. This will only happen if we purposefully leave their wants unfulfilled. This bears repeating: We cannot provide our children with everything they want or they will have no motivation whatsoever to work to earn money. Leaving some wants unfulfilled blesses the child.

Once they're motivated, we've created the perfect opportunity for them to learn to work hard at something. Jobs should be physically challenging: yard work, detail-cleaning a car, hauling sticks, washing garage windows. (Have you ever looked at how filthy garage windows can get?) The pay should be low but still motivating— $4.00/hour for a younger child or perhaps $6/hour for an older one. Insist on high-quality work. You are their boss, so expect good results for the money you're spending.

Resist the temptation to accept work that's incomplete or not detailed enough. Without being punitive or insulting, use these jobs as an opportunity to talk about being thorough, diligent and excellent. If you gave your child the job to clean out the car, then the job is finished only when the car looks clean and all cleaning supplies have been returned to where they belong.

Beware of Allowance Pitfalls

The most common and significant mistake parents make when it comes to allowance is giving their child too much money. The actual amount of the allowance doesn't matter as much as the amount that the child has full discretion in spending. For example, if parents give their 10-year-old son $10 a week with no requirements for saving some and giving some, then that child has enough money to buy 20 candy bars, five packs of baseball cards, a Nerf gun or a new stuffed animal each week. This seems more like a child learning to spend money randomly than a child learning to budget money.

Instead, let's see what could happen if those same parents give their son $10 a week, but they attach a few requirements (giving, saving, spending) to the allowance:

- Give $1.00 to church or a charity they believe in.
- Save $5.00 for college.
- Spend the remaining $4.00 as they wish. It should be enough to buy a treat or save for something at the end of the month.

However—and don't ignore this critical point—the parents must not buy the child additional treats during the month or else the allowance won't serve its purpose.

If the parents continue to stop at McDonalds when asked, pay for over-priced treats from the ice cream man, or buy a random toy at the store, then the allowance's primary function has been altered. Rather than giving kids an opportunity to make financial decisions, it becomes nothing more than a means to buy more stuff.

When considering what amount to give your children, think about:

- How much money do you want them to spend each week or month?
- What things will you be buying and what things will they be buying?
- If they want to go to an arcade with a friend, do they pay? If the family goes to the movies, who pays?

Younger children should start with less money and work their way up, while incrementally adding more expenses. When our children were younger and first getting started, I would still treat for the random family movie. As they grew older and received more money for their allowances, they needed to use their own money for the movies—or we split the cost. Do you want a trick for getting a teenager to bring a sibling to the movies? Offer to pay for the teen if he brings his younger sibling. It's like hiring a chaperone for the price of a movie ticket.

Another pitfall is the habit of giving kids a large amount of extra spending money for family vacations. It does make sense to have them earn or save a certain amount before a trip so that they won't be asking for things on the trip, but can you see how doing so could condition them? For one thing, it sends the message that vacations provide an opportunity to spend money on things you wouldn't buy at home. Kids make the connection that we are going on vacation to relax and have fun, so we'd better have extra money because fun costs money. It can quickly make the vacation into a quest for occasions to spend the saved (extra) money.

What if, instead, the focus of the vacation was to relax (which is free), to bond with family (free), and to explore new places (free or inexpensive)? What if we moved away from commercial-type vacations and toward exploring nature or enjoying an adventure together? What if kids brought some of their own money to spend but without the expectation that they need much more than they would spend at home?

Spender Vs. Saver

Using an allowance system also enables you to quickly identify whether your child is a spender or a saver. Even without an allowance this will probably be clear, but the allowance gives parents the chance to teach both of these types of kids skills they will need to learn in order to successfully navigate their financial futures.

The "spender" is the child who receives more joy in spending his money than in saving it. The "saver" simply enjoys the process of saving money more than he does spending it. Neither one is right or wrong—one is not better than the other. Each type of child will have something to learn through having an allowance.

The spender and the saver will always look at life differently. When my oldest two were about seven and eight, they had the opportunity to buy an ice cream bar at the neighborhood pool. After checking the price, the oldest (a spender) deemed it a good value. He immediately grabbed his "treat" spending money, bought the ice cream bar, and ate it with great joy. The younger of the two (saver) waited until the spender finished his ice cream before remarking, "Your ice cream bar is gone, and I still have 75 cents in my pocket."

To my younger "saver" son, the power to still choose what to spend his money on was of greater value than the ice cream bar itself. To my spender, the joy came in enjoying a cool, creamy treat on a hot day. Both were right. And both still have things they need to learn.

The spender must learn to take some of the firepower out of his pocket. He must learn the importance of delayed gratification, that he will appreciate things more if he waits for them. When my "spender" received his $1.00 a week at age five, he wanted to go shopping right away to exchange that crisp bill for a toy or treat. Something. Anything. Though we didn't immediately jump into the car, which would have served only to feed his addiction, he still talked about what he might buy until we finally went to the store. The thrill of that little toy lasted only until the following week when he got his next dollar.

The spender must also learn discernment. Some things that are cheap don't last very long. The Dollar Store and Target's dollar section are great places to teach the lesson that even though things seem like a "good deal," they aren't if they break. Cheap things are also not a good deal if the thrill in owning them doesn't last any longer than the day you bought them. Discuss these aspects after they make purchases in order to give the spender wise eyes—to help him see that so many things available for him to buy don't really bring joy beyond the initial rush of purchasing.

The saver must learn something very different. He must learn to find the joy that spending money wisely can bring. He must understand that because he'll need to spend money in his future, he needs to learn how to do it well. Often times, a saver feels guilty when he spends any money because he only wants to save it. He can be freed from this guilt when he learns to plan where he spends his money. Teach the saver to make a budget. As he gets more money and more responsibilities, he should include categories for treating himself and treating others. Then he can enjoy spending this money because it's part of the plan.

As adults, savers often struggle with spending money on anything other than basic necessities. They become paralyzed with the fear that they won't have enough money for the future. We worked with a number of folks who found freedom from this destructive place. In a marriage, often one spouse is the saver, so teaching that spouse how to spend responsibly can bring peace to many financial issues.

The "Almost-Ready-to-Launch" Allowance

When our oldest son, Michael, started his junior year in high school, we resolved to be even more intentional about the remaining months we had to train him to be financially wise as an adult. Within two years he would be on his own, managing the money he had been saving since age five, and he would be without our direct daily supervision. More than likely, those credit card applications and "free" t-shirts would be waiting for him on college registration day. We understood we had limited time for more intensive training.

Andy and I decided to give Michael the entire amount of money we would spend on him for the upcoming year. In the past he had received $15 a month for treat money and also managed $150 in September for back-to-school expenses and new clothes for the school year. We then paid the rest of his expenses throughout the year. Now, however, we proposed giving him all the money for the entire year: money for haircuts, school lunches, toiletries, sports fees, school fees, clothes, shoes, etc. Bottom line, we wanted to know: Was he ready to manage a large sum of money and make it last for the entire year?

His first step was to determine his annual expenses. He spent about a week itemizing all the things he would need for the year. We helped him brainstorm categories, but he came up with the dollar amounts under each category. He researched pricing on many things and asked tons of questions about my budget. We asked him to include $5 a month for treating friends to something so that he learned to be generous with people and to plan for his generosity.

When he completed his final budget, he presented it to us for approval. Most of the categories looked correct. He had included enough money for three movies a year, lunch at school once a week, eating out with friends once a month, etc. But the amount for haircuts seemed much more than I thought it should have been. When I questioned this expense, he produced the math of one haircut every 3-4 weeks at $15, which included a $3 tip. Because he had a buzz cut, his hair really was that expensive to maintain.

Once we approved his expenses, we moved the total amount of money for the year into a checking account for him. He was to use this account solely for the purpose of managing his annual budget. Any money from his job or gifts he received for his birthday or Christmas was to be kept in a separate account. This would enable him to see if he could truly manage his budget. Don't worry if you don't have the total amount available all at once. You could always move a specific amount into the account monthly.

It was a beautiful thing to watch this 17-year-old young man care so much about getting the best price for acne pads and shampoo. He quickly realized that if he found a coupon for $6.99 haircuts, then he suddenly had extra money to pay for ice cream bars at lunch that month. (He also learned that you calculate your tip from the price before the coupon.)

One of the best lessons he learned happened when I asked him to pay the $51 fee for taking the college admission test (SAT). "Hey, I can't pay for that! We didn't think of that in August when we did the budget. There isn't money in my account for that." Even though the account still had hundreds of dollars in it, Michael knew we had not put an additional $51 into the account for the test. I happily wrote the check for the SAT out of my account to celebrate his learning that even though he had money in the bank, he couldn't really "afford" the cost of the test.

We talked about how unplanned things will always come up; we taught him how to transfer needed funds from one account to another to cover them. I even had him figure out where he would have found the $51 from his current budget, if I had made him pay it. He figured out that he could have chosen to skip two haircuts, skip dinner out with friends, and pack his lunch the entire month. Almost every couple we ever met with for financial counseling had yet to learn this lesson. For so many people, money in the bank means they can afford to buy just about anything.

Michael also learned the importance of recording expenses and watching to see whether he was still "on track" each month. He also learned he could lump some of the categories into one and just call it "cash." This way he didn't need to keep track of money spent on a pack of gum or a pop at the gas station. He simply took out the same amount of money each month in cash, and he knew which categories it needed to cover. When he ran out of cash one month, he skipped going to a movie with friends because he wanted to stay on track and wait for the next month's cash.

Though many families track their monthly expenses, no family we counseled who experienced financial chaos met together monthly as a couple to see how the prior month's expenses turned out. Without evaluating where the money had actually gone, the couple blindly entered the next month, not knowing if they had gotten behind and needed to make adjustments for the next month. Help your children make this connection early and look at their monthly bank statement with them. Keep the atmosphere upbeat and encouraging. Allow them to ask questions and offer suggestions as needed. Remember, you're making the effort to ensure their future independence.

For entertainment, watch the program *30 for 30: Broke.* It tells the stories of a number of professional athletes who made millions but then lost it all. The tragic tales motivate kids to learn how to be financially wise because no amount of income will ever be enough for the person who does not know how to manage a budget and live within their means.

Because of all the training we had done leading up to this ready-to-launch allowance, Michael made his money last until the next August when he resubmitted his new budget, which included money to take the SAT again. This allowance system succeeded because of the incremental steps we took along the way and the culture in our home concerning money and possessions.

If you have an older teen with minimal experience budgeting money, I would take immediate steps to remedy the situation.

1. Stop being your child's personal ATM. (No money for movies, treats, dates, activities with friends. None.)
2. Open a bank account with them.
3. Insist they start earning money and saving half of it for their future. (This money stays in the bank until they leave the house for college or to live on their own.)
4. If they've never had an allowance, give them a small amount (the price of two movie tickets) and insist they save 25% of it in their new account.
5. Have them read the letter to teens in the back of this book.
6. Within six months, consider giving them access to a larger amount of money. Help them create a budget and talk with them about tracking it each month.

Building a Financial Foundation

The primary role of an allowance is to help children learn basic principles that will serve as a strong foundation for their financial futures. The first lesson is that money has three primary functions.

- To give to others
- To save for short term or long-term goals

- To spend on current needs or desires

This idea of give/save/spend is foundational. Without this concept, it's all too easy for kids to believe that money exists solely for spending on themselves, which is the message our culture pounds into them. Use your children's allowance to coach them to "give some, save some, spend some." Some people recommend specific percentages, but Andy and I have concerned ourselves more with simply establishing the habit of giving some money to others and saving some money in the bank regularly.

As soon as we started an allowance with each of our boys, we also opened a bank account for them at the local bank. This account enabled us (and our sons) to deposit money for college, money they couldn't take out. Not only could they save a few dollars from their allowances once a month, but they could also deposit birthday money from relatives. With interest rates for saving accounts at an all-time low, we chose to give them an incentive with our own interest rate of 15% as well as some parental money incentives when their accounts reached $250 and $1,000; these enticed them to keep the savings account growing. When the boys each reached $1,500, we also presented them with a special knife that they still treasure today.

Marketers have created a variety of piggy banks kids can use to put money into three separate give/save/spend sections, but, in my opinion, spending money on these sort of defeats the point. Instead of purchasing a ready-made product, work with your child to make his or her own. I would also encourage them to add a special jar for saving up spending money for a short time so they can buy something that costs more than a few dollars. By having your children do this themselves, they'll take even more ownership of the project and the resulting habits.

Allowances can also teach the lesson of delayed gratification. Kids need to hone the critical skill of learning to wait for something rather than acting on impulses. Many adults fail to wait before buying something they want. Not buying your kids anything outside of birthdays and Christmases forces them to wait for a gift-buying occasion to get a toy or to save their own money over a period of time. If they never delay gratification, they see only how quickly the money is gone and how short-lasting the thrill of the purchase really is.

Finally, when parents give kids their "own" money, the kids tend to take more responsibility for it and feel more connected to it. Most kids take extra care when spending their own money on something rather than when they spend their parent's money. It's quite common to hear a child request a toy or a snack at the store, but when mom suggests he use his own money, he instantly (and "magically") is no longer interested.

Another side benefit of the allowance system we used was that our kids quickly learned how much things cost. This not only included groceries and shoes, but also new carpet, an oil change and a gallon of paint. An allowance gave them a reference point and a heightened interest in how much things cost. As my oldest son witnessed me writing a check to the dentist one day, he remarked, "Wow, thanks for paying for me to get my teeth cleaned." The receptionist admitted that was the first time she had heard a child thank their parent for a dental cleaning.

An allowance can teach or it can spoil. It can empower or it can weaken. Take care and plan with your spouse how to best use this tool so your kids benefit in the long run. Use personal responsibility, chores, and jobs to develop a strong work ethic and enhance the lessons learned when coupled with the allowance. Your kids will move out of your house one day. I encourage you to train them for a financial future that will enable them to live with contentment at any income level. They will thank you for this gift.

CHAPTER 14

THE JOY OF GIVING

We've reached the end. The last chapter. But I feel like I've saved the best for last. It is so much more gratifying to write and read about giving than about materialism. Giving is the antithesis of materialism. It's the antidote. We can't worship our money and possessions while we give them away. Generosity brings us joy. A recently published book on marketing and fundraising called *The Science of Giving* conducted numerous studies to prove what we already know in our hearts, "Giving makes people happy." The researchers concluded the following:

1. Giving makes you happy. People who committed random acts of kindness were significantly happier than those who didn't, and spending money on others makes you happier than spending money on yourself.
2. Happier people help others more, and they give more. A positive mood makes you nicer.
3. This creates a circular cycle: giving makes you happy, and when you're happy you give more, which makes you happier, which makes you give more.[1]

The opposite is true when people focus on possessions, status, and stuff. Author and psychologist Madeline Levine, begins her book, *The Price of Privilege*, with a story I will never forget about one of her teenage clients:

> *I slumped into my well-worn chair feeling depleted and surprisingly close to tears. The 15-year-old who had just left my office was bright, personable, highly pressured by her adoring, but frequently preoccupied, affluent parents, and very angry. She had used a razor to incise the word EMPTY on her left forearm, showing it to me when I commented on her typical cutter disguise—a long-sleeve t-shirt pulled halfway over her hand, with an opening torn in the cuff for her thumb.*[2]

Why in the world would a teenager feel this empty at such a young age? Perhaps this young girl was so angry because the things she had been chasing to fill her up and provide her with security and significance had instead only left her feeling unfulfilled. Perhaps her preoccupied parents only noticed the surface of their bright, personable daughter rather than connecting with her on a deep level. Perhaps she was created to be in relationship with her Creator and her soul yearned for that connection.

We have been created for relationships. In particular, we have been created to have a deep and personal relationship with God through Jesus Christ His son. When we find this relationship, our lives are reoriented and our focus shifts from ourselves to Him. Jesus Christ becomes Enough for us. Psalm 23 begins, "The Lord is my Shepherd, I lack nothing." No longer do Christ followers have to feel the emptiness of this world. Everything changes when we are reconciled to God though Jesus Christ.

One way God leads us away from the pain of materialism toward "lacking nothing" is through generosity to others. By giving our money and material possessions to others in need, we devalue their importance and their significance in our own lives, and we allow ourselves to enjoy the internal blessings of giving. We recognize the false promises of money and possessions. Would the teenage girl above have felt less empty if she had been generous with both her money and her time? Would connecting with others in this way have saved her some pain and loneliness? Giving is simply a part of living.

We Give because He Gave

When you begin to succeed in the financial lifestyle presented in this book, it can be easy to lose sight of the big picture and instead get caught in the details. Instead of working with your family to create contentment, you could become the warden of the checkbook. Instead of saving money so that you will be free to serve others, saving can become an end in itself.

I have a friend who, because of health problems and poor choices, has lived in poverty for the past decade or more. As she began to apply these principles of Enough to her life, and as her financial situation began to improve, she instinctively began to clutch her assets more tightly. The more money she got, the less she wanted to give it away.

And then God gave her a really big gift. For years, she and her family had been stuck in a house without basic amenities. The plumbing in the bathroom didn't work, the water was not drinkable, and the house was literally falling apart around them. Their landlord refused to do any repairs, but because they had poor credit and no assets, they could not move anywhere else. My friend was completely unable to change her situation with her own power.

One day, she and her husband received a phone call asking them to come see a house that was for sale. A generous donor knew of their plight and was willing to give them a personal loan so that they could have a real home. Never in their wildest dreams did my friend imagine that *this* was the way their problem would be solved. She wondered: Was the offer for real? Would there be strings attached?

Surely this was too good to be true. But the offer was genuine, and they were able to escape their dire situation with a loan payment much less than their former rent payment.

They are now settled in their new home. It has *two* working bathrooms and the house is clean and cozy. Every day when she wakes up, or when she makes dinner for her family, or when she comes home from work, my friend is reminded that *everything* she has was given to her. It isn't because she worked hard or planned for the future or saved every penny. In the end, it was God's provision and the generosity of one of His servants that rescued her.

Now my friend is eager to give. Not only is she learning how to give of her money, but she also actively searches for ways to share the gifts God has provided by offering her home as a place of warmth and refuge to friends and neighbors.

Though many of us might not have such a striking example of God's provision in our lives, the truth is that we all depend on God for everything we have. He is a God who "did not spare his own Son, but gave him up for us all, [so] how will he not also, along with him, graciously give us all things?" (Romans 8:32). Reflect on that. God gave up what was most precious to Him so that we might be rescued. And everything good that we have comes from Him. He gave so that we might have freedom. It is in that freedom that we are now able to gratefully give.

The Gift of Service

Quite often, people forget that generosity is not just about giving money and gifts, but it includes our time also. Before I had kids, I visited a nursing home with my dog as part of pet therapy for the residents. Sure, they liked Cody, my border collie, but once I started having kids and bringing them to visit, the residents *loved* them. Because I brought them from the time they were babies, my boys were never afraid of the sights and sounds and smells of the home.

Visiting a nursing home became something they thought every kid did on a Sunday afternoon.

Service opportunities abound for kids of any age—even preschoolers can participate in family or church projects. Some small groups from our church "adopt" an older person who needs help periodically keeping up their yards and gardens. Though the younger kids might not be as much help as the teenagers, they still feel a part of the group and the older people especially love to interact with them.

But giving and serving don't have to be isolated to official church-or school-sponsored events. Teach your kids the invaluable phrase, "What can I do to help you?" Not only will this bless their spouses one day, but it will bless the child who can learn to seek and find opportunities to serve. Help them notice others and how they might help:

- offer an older person their seat
- clean up after a meal at a friend's house
- help someone struggling with a task
- offer to get something someone needs
- help a teacher quiet a class
- give away a toy or clothes that someone else would need or enjoy more

Developing an Eye for Giving Opportunities

Similar training can be done to help kids develop an eye for opportunities to donate their money earmarked for giving. Just like they gained an eye for recognizing junk, kids can also recognize a situation where they can help by giving money. At the beginning you will need to offer suggestions, but quickly they begin to see these situations themselves.

I remember when Christopher was in kindergarten and we were dropping off canned food at the neighborhood pantry. He noticed all the children who were waiting with their parents to pick up their bags of canned corn and beans. Convicted, he asked if he could use his giving money to buy lollipops and pass them out to the kids who were waiting in the line. He also wanted to use his money to buy cookies for them to take home. His one-man mission became making sure kids had sugary treats in their house along with the healthy food. Similarly, Bryan decided to buy dog treats for the puppies at the Humane Society. A few other giving opportunities include:

- Folders/crayons/notebooks for kids in need
- Cake mix and icing for special birthday bags at the food pantry
- Popsicles for a single mom to pass out to neighborhood kids
- A scarf for a cancer patient
- New toys for a Christmas giving tree
- Dog toys at the Humane Society
- Baby mittens for a women's shelter
- Wrapping paper to wrap donated gifts
- A book for a teacher's classroom
- A sandwich and fries for a homeless man
- Bingo prizes at a nursing home

With allowances so small by design (see chapter 13), it's sometimes fun to let them see their gifts be literally multiplied to do even bigger things. Remind them that giving is a habit, and that Jesus taught about how God blesses the act of giving, so any gift can be multiplied by God to do good work. But parents can also partner with them in this endeavor and offer to multiply their gifts. For every dollar they give away, you can add $4 more so they can decide where to donate the $5 gift.

Be ready. Some kids might get so excited about the matching gift that they will offer to work for extra money and give away $10 or $20 of their own money. It's always best to set the parameters ahead of time, while also being ready to give extravagantly so they can witness what their gifts can do. Organizations like World Vision and Compassion International offer catalogs around Christmas time where kids can peruse the pages for gifts benefitting kids living in poverty around the globe. Some favorites with my kids include two chicks for $25 or five ducks for $35. These gifts can then be given in honor of a relative, so Grandpa can share in your child's joy of giving rather than receiving another pair of slippers for Christmas.

The Joy of Giving

Years ago, when all four boys were still very young, they decided to use their giving money to buy prizes for the weekly bingo game at the nursing home. Michael came up with the idea when he noticed that the prizes the residents could win were minimal by his standards: a banana, a can of Sprite, deodorant, some magazines. He rallied his brothers to save up their giving money so together they would right this wrong in the world. I have vivid memories of all of us in Wal-Mart carefully choosing prizes. After literally an hour, Michael finally chose a large stuffed dog, Bryan decided on a heart-shaped necklace, Christopher chose a watch, and Matthew found a bright pink scarf.

The next week the boys were giddy with anticipation about whose prize would be chosen first. They placed their treasures alongside the usual prizes on the cart. They waited expectantly as the game began. Within seconds after 82-year-old Esther shouted, "Bingo," the boys rushed the cart over to her so she could select her prize. All four quickly marketed their prize for her to consider. She looked. She touched. She said, "Oh my, that's beautiful." Then she chose the banana—surprising both the boys and me with the reality of what is truly valued when you have lived so many decades.

A parenting magazine I read a few years ago asked readers this question: "We'd all like to give our kids as many luxuries as possible, but many worry that they'll take them for granted. Do you think your child is spoiled?" My concern here is not the answer to the question but rather the question itself. Really? We would *all* like to give our kids as many luxuries as possible? Well, I wouldn't. And I would hope that after reading this book, you wouldn't either.

Let me put it this way. I love mint chocolate chip ice cream. My kids love mint chocolate chip ice cream. But would I really like to give them as much ice cream as possible? No. It wouldn't be good for them. The answer is obvious. Then why is it so challenging for us to apply the same logic to material possessions? Giving our kids "as many luxuries as possible" is not good for them or for us.

Inoculate your family from the dangers of our materialistic culture. Nurture your children and cultivate their hearts for giving and serving. Develop strong family bonds that will keep the materialistic culture outside the walls of your home. Bravely become counter-cultural. Say no to excess. Stand firm in your convictions to provide your family with a gift that will help them become grateful for everything they have—the gift of Enough.

~∞∞∞~

There was one more lesson to be learned at the nursing home that afternoon the woman chose the banana as her bingo prize. During the third round of bingo a resident finally selected one of the prizes the boys had so painstakingly picked out. A sweet, older lady with vein-gnarled, yet manicured hands thoughtfully selected the large stuffed dog. (This would not have been my first choice, but then again neither would the banana.)

Michael was quite pleased that his prize had been chosen first, confirming in his mind that he selected the best one. But then the lady did something that surprised us both. She gave Michael the stuffed dog. "I would like for you to take this dog home and enjoy him. I can tell how much you like it."

What this woman wanted more than the jewelry or treats was the ability to give. She wanted to feel the joy someone feels when they're able to make another person happy. Having lived over eighty years, this woman, whose possessions had been reduced to what would fit into a ten by ten foot room, didn't want any more stuff. She wanted the joy that the stuff couldn't bring.

Despite a decade of purging unwanted toys and stuffed animals in our home, this dog remains as a reminder about the innate joy of giving. The tattered stuffed dog reminds our entire family that when all the birthdays and book fairs, carnivals and Christmases, vacations and staycations are over—what we have left is the joy we receive from our relationships with people, and our ability to give.

Afterword

Final Unsolicited Advice from a Stranger

I guess I am no longer a stranger after you have read so many stories about my family and me. I hope you have enjoyed them and have collected a few ideas along the way. I'd like to leave you with a warning. Now that you have recently finished the book, you might be tempted to fall into one of two traps:

1) You may become so overwhelmed with the amount of training you still need to do with your kids that you remain fearfully paralyzed.
2) Or you may become so overconfident with the new information in your hands that you go on parenting auto-pilot while using some of these ideas.

I hope you do neither...

If trap #1 sounds possible, please remember that no matter how much your kids may love their stuff or how little they may know about Enough right now, there is plenty of time for improvement. Don't attempt to completely revamp your lifestyle. Instead, make small changes:

- declutter one area
- purge five things

- stop all Mom ATM withdrawals
- start saying "no" more often
- talk about the power of stuff to bring discontentment
- maximize your family time to nurture a place where everyone feels known and loved.

Also remember that you are only human. You may have been feeling some guilt about things you have done in the past to create discontentment in your home. But hold my hand and say this with me: We all make mistakes!—Many of the examples in this book came from my own mistakes, yet I still wrote the book. Give yourself grace.

Feel free to use my go-to statement for times when I realize I have missed something in the parenting arena and need to make a change: "Hey, Dad and I have started to notice that you are having a hard time figuring out _____. I think it would be more helpful if he and I started _____ so that you can break this habit before you are an adult.

If trap #2 sounds more appealing, I want to remind you that there are no exact formulas for raising financially wise kids. Kids can have a decade of wise teaching and still be tempted to follow the allure of our materialistic culture. Recently, I counseled a young man in his twenties who had left college prematurely to chase a high paying job. He lived well for a little while, but then the job ended abruptly leaving him with no income and a stack of debts.

As I talked to him about minimizing expenses, saving, planning, and digging out of debt, he kept repeating: "My parents taught me that." "Oh, I know about that from what my parents showed me." His parents had poured a solid foundation, but for a time, this man chose the foolish path. Yet the teachings of his parents enabled him to make progress quickly and begin to right his past mistakes.

This is the reality of parenting. We have a role to teach our kids what is right, but we can't take full responsibility for the adults they will become one day. We are taught in Proverbs 22 to "start children off on the way they should go..." But then we must trust the power of the Holy Spirit to convict their hearts and finish the work we began.

You and I may not know each other yet, but please understand that we are on this journey together. And there are others like us. My website/blog at **mariannemiller.com** provides helpful resources but more importantly a community of other parents who are seeking a different way forward for our kids—one where gratitude replaces materialism every time. Join us there and tell me your story!

A LETTER FOR YOUR TEENAGER

Hi tween or teen!

Hi! I'm the author of the book your parents have been reading. I appreciate you taking your time to read this letter. I wrote the book to help make sure kids like you don't become adults like the ones I counsel about their money. Many of them are doctors or high-ranking business people. Many have attended colleges like Harvard and Stanford. But their jobs and degrees haven't saved them; they are all in big trouble with their money. They experience great stress. They argue with their spouses and kids. They feel like they're in bondage.

So how did they get there? Why was even a $300,000 annual income not enough for some? Why were so many of these people driving expensive cars but not able to really afford them? The bank actually owned their cars, and these high-income earners owned merely the stress of the debt. Believe me, seeing the pain and pressure they were under shocked and saddened me. Lots of kids your age want to be "rich" when they grow up. What these kids don't realize is that they will *never* be rich, if they don't first understand how much is Enough.

Many people can make a lot of money, but if they also have a lot of debt too, then they are not really rich. Rather they are like slaves to the debt. Banks and credit card companies control them and hold their freedom. These people cannot enjoy a good night's sleep because they lay awake in the grip of worry. They don't have the freedom to change jobs if they wanted to because they can't go two weeks without a paycheck. They feel trapped—and indeed they are.

But you don't have to live like that. Your parents have taken a stand and are making a purposeful effort to help you create habits that will ensure your freedom as an adult. They want to help you be free to take any job you want and to live a life free of financial stress.

Let me tell you how they plan to help you. The first step is to be sure you don't develop a See-and-Spend habit. Many kids your age have made a habit out of wanting almost everything they see that looks the least bit appealing. At a baseball game, they want a hot pretzel at the snack bar even though they are not hungry. At the zoo, they want a tattoo of a lion painted on their face. In the cafeteria at school, they grab a Gatorade every day even though it costs a dollar fifty, and the milk would have been free. If their friend gets a cute new sweatshirt for her birthday, they now want one too. You get the idea.

Consumerism (buying a lot of stuff all the time) is a habit that can destroy lives. We live in a culture where advertisers prey on unsuspecting kids and adults by creating a need or a desire and then offering their product to fulfill that desire. Don't be one of their victims by continuing to wish, desire, dream, and buy.

The Bible says, "Whoever loves money never has enough; whoever loves wealth will never be satisfied with his income" (Ecc. 5:10). Don't you want to have Enough? A bucket with holes in it can never be filled up no matter how much water is poured inside. Likewise, a person who has insatiable desires can never make enough money to satisfy themselves.

So please pay attention to your day-to-day experiences. Your parents will be doing their best *not* to give you everything you want because they do not want you to grow into an adult who cannot be satisfied with the basics. They love you and want you to be an adult who is not in trouble financially. When you move out of your parents' house one day, you will need to know how to live with limited income. That's called "getting started." If you get in the habit now of buying whatever you want, you will never have enough money to pay your bills in the future. It might seem like fun now, but it won't be fun later. And later lasts a lot longer than the present.

The second thing is to be sure you understand the importance of saving. I heard a teenager once say that teens *should* spend everything they earn now because, when they are older, they won't be able to. That is really bad advice. Actually now is the only time in your life when you don't have to pay your own bills with your own money. So if you earn money now, you have the chance to save a lot of money for when you are older.

The people we helped with their money problems didn't understand the importance of saving money. They planned to save all the "leftover" money, but without careful planning, they rarely have any leftover money to save. The key to having money for savings is to make a budget. Even multi-million dollar companies have to budget their money. Budgets are definitely not just for people with only a little money. They definitely aren't bad. They will actually help you and keep you free.

I like to think of budgets as protected swim areas at the beach or at a lake. The ropes indicate to the swimmers where it's safe to swim. Lifeguards can watch them there. No boats can enter this area. But if a swimmer swims beyond the ropes, lifeguards can no longer protect them. It just doesn't make sense to take risks like that.

Even as a teen, you can practice budgeting by deciding to devote a certain percentage of your money to a savings account and a certain percentage to help others. The rest you can spend, but I would even divide that money into "pocket money," entertainment money, and luxury purchases (a cool watch or new shoes). Those basics will help you begin to control your money so it never controls you.

Finally, debt equals bondage. Debt is like slavery. Debt is simply money you spend that you don't even have yet. Debt relies on the future, which is completely unknown. Banks and credit card companies *love* to loan you money for houses, cars, clothes and even groceries. They don't care what you buy with it because they make their money back regardless of how you spend it.

Let me explain this in more detail with a quick example: Kelsey decides to splurge on some back-to-school clothes at the mall. She charges $500 worth of cute outfits on a credit card. When the bill comes the following month, however, she still doesn't have enough money to pay for the clothes. So she pays just a little bit. They call it a minimum payment. By the time she eventually pays off the loan a couple years later, she will have paid nearly $1000 and the outfits will be at Goodwill. She spent $500 on clothes, but she also spent $500 on interest fees to the bank. She got nothing for that additional $500—except a lot of headaches and worry. Owing money to other people keeps you in bondage because you spend chunks of your money paying for things that you *have* to pay for rather than deciding what things you *want* to pay.

Here are a few final action points:

- Make a commitment now that you will never go into credit card debt.
- Think more about what you really want to *do* when you're an adult rather than just how much money you want to *make*. Big paychecks do not equal big happiness. People who love their jobs (no matter the pay) are the happiest.
- Start saving money for the future *you* in the bank. I'm quite sure that you will thank yourself when you're older.
- Pay attention to what things you buy with your money or your parents' money. Can you just save that money instead?

- Consider how much stuff you already have. Do you appreciate it? Are you grateful for it? Is it enough? If it's not, then how much is enough?

That's really about all there is to it. Your mom and dad want you to be happy. They want you to be able to live on your own. They love you and will do what they need to do to help you learn how to control your money so that it never controls you.

Thanks for reading,
Marianne Miller

END NOTES

Chapter 2: The Joneses are Broke

1   Sinclair, Upton. *The Jungle*. Cambridge, MA: R. Bentley, 1971. Print.
2   New International Version (NIV) Holy Bible, New International Version®, NIV® Copyright © 1973, 1978, 1984, 2011 by Biblica, Inc.® Used by permission. All rights reserved worldwide.
3   Peterson, Christopher, Ph.D. "Who Most Enjoy the Small Things in Life?" *Psychology Today: Health, Help, Happiness + Find a Therapist*. N.p., 1 June 2010. Web. 12 Sept. 2014.
4   Nivene. "CashNetUSA Annual Survey." *CashNetUSA Blog*. N.p., 19 June 2013. Web. 9 Aug. 2014.

Chapter 3: A Culture of Consumerism

1   "Living beyond Your Means? Live within Your Budget." *Living beyond Your Means? Live within Your Budget*. N.p., n.d. Web. 2 July 2014.
2   "Videos for Students." *Welcome to CARE, Your Financial Literacy Resource*. N.p., n.d. Web. 8 June 2014.
3   "Videos for Students." Welcome to CARE, Your Financial Literacy Resource. N.p., n.d. Web. 8 June 2014.

Chapter 4: The Power of the Family

1   FitzGerald, Susan. "'Crack Baby' Study Ends with Unexpected but Clear Result." *Philly.com*. N.p., 22 July 2013. Web. 2 June 2014.

2   Brooks, Robert B., and Sam Goldstein. *Raising Resilient Children: Fostering Strength, Hope, and Optimism in Your Child*. Lincolnwood, IL: Contemporary, 2001. Print.

3   Carter, Christine. *Raising Happiness: 10 Simple Steps for More Joyful Kids and Happier Parents*. New York: Ballantine, 2010. Print

4   Pipher, Mary Bray. *The Shelter of Each Other: Rebuilding Our Families*. New York: G.P. Putnam's Sons, 1996. Print.

5   Tarkan, Laurie. "Benefits of the Dinner Table Ritual." *The New York Times*. The New York Times, 02 May 2005. Web. 2 June 2014.

6   Weinstein, Miriam. *The Surprising Power of Family Meals: How Eating Together Makes Us Smarter, Stronger, Healthier, and Happier*. Hanover, NH: Steerforth, 2005. Print.

7   Dolin, Ann. "How Family Dinners Improve Students' Grades - Private Tutoring and Test Prep - Educational Connections." *Private Tutoring and Test Prep Educational Connections*. N.p., n.d. Web. 5 July 2014.

8   Dobson, James. "Families at The Dinner Table." *Families at The Dinner Table*. N.p., n.d. Web. 5 July 2014.

Chapter 5: Fighting for Influence

1   Pipher, Mary Bray. *The Shelter of Each Other: Rebuilding Our Families*. New York: G.P. Putnam's Sons, 1996. Print.

2   DeGaetano, Gloria. *Parenting Well in a Media Age: Keeping Our Kids Human*. Fawnskin, CA: Personhood, 2004. Print.

3   Kasser, Tim. *The High Price of Materialism*. Cambridge, MA: MIT, 2002. Print.

4   Kroeker, Ann S. *Not so Fast: Slow-down Solutions for Frenzied Families*. Colorado Springs, CO: David C. Cook, 2009. Print.

5   Kasser, Tim. *The High Price of Materialism*. Cambridge, MA: MIT, 2002. Print.

Chapter 6: The Gift of Enough

1   Snyder, Michael. "America Has Highest Divorce Rate Obesity Rate Depression Rate - Google Search." *America Has Highest Divorce Rate Obesity Rate Depression Rate - Google Search.* N.p., 23 Apr. 2013. Web. 5 July 2014.

2   Stanley, Thomas J., and William D. Danko. *The Millionaire next Door: The Surprising Secrets of America's Wealthy.* Atlanta, GA: Longstreet, 1996. Print.

3   Zagier, Allan. "Lottery Winners Share Lessons, Risks of a Giant Powerball Prize - DailyFinance." *DailyFinance.com.* N.p., 28 Nov. 2012. Web. 3 Aug. 2014.

4   Haisley, Emily. *Loving a Bad Bet.* Pittsburg: Carnegie Mellon University, Mar. 2008. Pdf.

Chapter 7: Managing Their Environment

1   McLeod, Sam. "Pavlov's Dogs | Simply Psychology." *Pavlov's Dogs | Simply Psychology.* N.p., Jan. 2013. Web. 11 June 2014.

Chapter 9: Creating a Financial Filter

1   Logorio, Christine. "Resources: Marketing To Kids." *CBSNews.* CBS Interactive, 14 May 2007. Web. 5 July 2014.

Chapter 10: The Power of Stuff

1   Schor, Juliet. *Born to Buy: The Commercialized Child and the New Consumer Culture.* New York: Scribner, 2004. Print.

2   Myers, David G. *The Pursuit of Happiness: Who Is Happy—and Why.* New York: W. Morrow, 1992. Print.

3   DeGaetano, Gloria. *Parenting Well in a Media Age: Keeping Our Kids Human.* Fawnskin, CA: Personhood, 2004. Print.

4   Velez-Mitchell, Jane, and Sandra Mohr. *Addict Nation: An Intervention for America.* Deerfield Beach, FL: Health Communications, 2011. Print.

Chapter 11: Delaying Gratification

1   Clear, James. "40 Years of Stanford Research Found That People With This One Quality Are More Likely to Succeed." *James Clear*. N.p., n.d. Web. 12 July 2014.

Chapter 12: Preparing Them for Poverty

1   Shah, Anup. "Poverty Facts and Stats." - *Global Issues*. N.p., 7 Jan. 2013. Web. 5 July 2014.

2   "Global Rich List." *Global Rich List*. N.p., n.d. Web. 15 Feb. 2014.

3   Kasser, Tim. *The High Price of Materialism*. Cambridge, MA: MIT, 2002. Print.

4   Ramsey, Dave. *The Total Money Makeover: A Proven Plan for Financial Fitness*. Nashville: Thomas Nelson Pub., 2003. Print.

5   "The Ultimate Allowance." *The Ultimate Allowance*. N.p., n.d. Web. 5 July 2014.

Chapter 14: The Joy of Giving

1   Oppenheimer, Daniel M., and Christopher Yves Olivola. *The Science of Giving: Experimental Approaches to the Study of Charity*. New York: Psychology, 2011. Print.

2   Levine, Madeline. *The Price of Privilege: How Parental Pressure and Material Advantage Are Creating a Generation of Disconnected and Unhappy Kids*. New York: HarperCollins, 2006. Print.